AFTER MY LAI

After My Lai

MY YEAR COMMANDING FIRST PLATOON, CHARLIE COMPANY

GARY W. BRAY

University of Oklahoma Press : Norman

This book is published with the generous assistance of The Wallace C. Thompson Endowment Fund, University of Oklahoma Foundation.

Library of Congress Cataloging-in-Publication Data

Bray, Gary W.
   After My Lai : my year commanding First Platoon, Charlie Company / Gary W. Bray. — 1st ed.
      p. cm.
   ISBN 978-0-8061-4045-2 (pbk. : alk. paper)   1. Bray, Gary W.
2. Vietnam War, 1961–1975—Personal narratives, American
3. Vietnam War, 1961–1975—Campaigns—Vietnam, Northern.
4. Soldiers—Oklahoma—Biography.   I. Title.
   DS559.5.B738 2009
   959.704'342092—dc22

                                                          2009002589

The paper in this book meets the guidelines for permanence and durability of the Committee on Production Guidelines for Book Longevity of the Council on Library Resources, Inc. ∞

1 2 3 4 5 6 7 8 9 10

To the memory of

Dennis Harold Guthrie
Quinton, Oklahoma
Killed in action January 23, 1969
Age 19

Ronald Eugene Embree
Thurman, Iowa
Killed in action January 9, 1970
Age 20

Boyd Lee Wade
Ringling, Oklahoma
Killed in action January 9, 1970
Age 23

Sherman Felton Armstrong
Poteau, Oklahoma
Killed in action August 14, 1970
Age 21

Contents

Illustrations

FIGURES

All photographs are from the author's collection, unless otherwise noted in the caption.

MAP

Preface

This story is about a young man who grew up in eastern Oklahoma during the 1950s and 1960s. Along with the other young men of my generation, I was confronted with America's involvement in the Vietnam War. Shortly after graduating from high school in 1967, I joined the army. My decision to enlist was heavily influenced by my association with family members who had served in World War II. I especially admired my uncle Olen, who had been wounded and decorated for valor.

I went to war as all young men go, ignorant of the things I was about to face. All of my preconceived notions of what war would be like were quickly shattered. I arrived in Vietnam in the fall of 1969 as a second lieutenant six months out of officer candidate school. I was assigned command of the platoon formerly led by Lt. William Calley, who a little over a year earlier had been primarily responsible for the My Lai massacre, in which close to five hundred Vietnamese women, old men, and children were murdered.

During the year I spent in Vietnam as a platoon leader, I experienced every emotion that can occur in war. I experienced sadness and horror as I watched the young men of my platoon die and be maimed. I experienced friendship no man can ever know until he shares the hardships of war with his fellow soldiers. I experienced

hatred and contempt for the people we were supposed to be helping. Most important, I experienced an event known as the Vietnam
War. America would like to forget that chapter of its history, but
those of us who were involved in it will never be able to forget it. It
is the dominant event of our lives. Marriage, children, or careers are
what most people consider to be the defining aspects of their lives.
For us, Vietnam will move aside only when we draw our last breath.

All of the events of this story are true. I have made no attempt to
embellish them or make them more interesting or exciting. The dia-
logue is as close as I can remember, considering the circumstances
and passage of years. In conversations after the events with two soldiers, Len Groom and Tony Nunes, their memories of what happened to our platoon concurred with mine. My hope is that the
reader will come away from this book with a better understanding of
the long-term effects of sending young men off to war. I have no
regrets for serving my country. I would do it again in an instant. My
only regret is that some of the boys of my platoon didn't make it
home.

When my wife, Joyce, and I retired in 1998, I began to consider
writing about my experiences in Vietnam. I had never really talked
to anyone about them except her, and writing a book seemed a fit-
ting way to honor the memory of my friends who had died there. If
nothing else, it would give my children a better understanding of
something that had so dramatically shaped my life as a young man.

Saying that you are going to write a book and doing so are two
completely different things. I worked on the story for six years. During the first four years, I became so discouraged with my efforts that
several times I put the manuscript away for six months or more. In
2004 I made up my mind either to finish the book or to abandon it
completely. I began to read through the many letters I had written
home to my wife while overseas. I ordered copies of First Battalion,
Twentieth Infantry's S-3 daily journals from the National Archives
and Record Administration in College Park, Maryland. Any time

anything of significance happened to platoons in Vietnam, they sent that information to their battalion headquarters. The information was recorded in these daily logs, which served as primary sources for this work.

I also obtained from the National Archives the U.S. Army's preliminary investigation into the My Lai incident, dated March 14, 1970, which was my primary source for the material included here about the My Lai massacre. *Four Hours in My Lai*, by Michael Bilton and Kevin Sim, also provided much valuable information concerning the My Lai tragedy. For those who would try to understand what happened that morning in March 1968, when young American soldiers became brutal dealers of death, the book gives an in-depth and disturbing account of the events leading up to and during that fatal morning. Information for chapter 4, "Charlie Company's Taste of War," came from the battalion's S-3 daily journals and conversations with members of my platoon who experienced the event, especially Tony Nunes.

Perhaps the most fortunate thing I did was to contact the woman who had taught my four children English in high school. I owe Carolyn Benham a debt of gratitude that I can never repay for her endless hours of reading and editing my primitive writing.

Finally, I owe my wife and children dearly for putting up with so much that had to do with Vietnam.

AFTER MY LAI

Ringling, Oklahoma, 2002 I

A cold north wind cut across the southern Oklahoma countryside as my wife and I drove eastward along the narrow two-lane highway. The barren trees along the fencerows swayed back and forth in the cold wind that blew over the fields of green wheat. We were celebrating our thirty-fourth wedding anniversary by taking a weekend trip to the western part of the state to visit the little community of Hollister where she had gone to school as a girl. The old school had been torn down and all that remained of it was the front façade where the entrance had been. Next to the school, the old, white wood-framed house where her family had lived was abandoned and falling down, but she enjoyed showing me the places where she had played as a little girl and pointing out where her childhood friends had lived.

As we passed through a small town on our way back home, a green road sign read "Ringling 10 miles." I had heard many stories about Ringling, and I had watched as the boy who told them to me died. I remembered him wading in a river in Vietnam, on what was called the Gaza Strip, telling me about this place. As we neared the small town, another green sign on a gravel road to the right read "Ceme-tery." I told my wife that I wanted to stop at the cemetery to find the boy's grave. We drove into town and stopped at a small store. I asked the young girl behind the cash register if that was the only cemetery

3

in Ringling. She informed me that she was sorry, but she lived in another town and wasn't sure. As I left the store, an old man pulled up and got out of his truck. I asked him if he lived in Ringling.

"All my life," he said.

I asked him if the cemetery I had passed coming into town was the community's only one, and he said that it was. I asked him if he had known a boy by the name of Boyd Wade who was killed in Vietnam. I told him that I had been the boy's platoon leader and would like to visit his grave. The old man said he remembered Boyd and thought that he was buried in the northeast part of the cemetery. I thanked him, and my wife and I drove back out of town to the cemetery.

As we entered the main gate of the graveyard, the first thing I noticed was a large granite monument in the center of the road, which read, "Dedicated to those who served." The monument listed the men buried in the cemetery who had served in the military. In the column of names on the right side, Boyd Wade was listed with a small star next to his name. The star indicated that he had been killed in action.

We drove up and down the gravel lanes looking for the monument that marked his grave. We had searched nearly all the cemetery when, as I looked out the car window, his headstone suddenly appeared: "Boyd Lee Wade, January 9, 1970." I slowly opened the car door. There were no other people around. It was quiet, as only a cemetery can be, with the cold north wind blowing through leafless trees. A small American flag fluttered in the wind.

My eyes began to water as I neared the grave. Must be the cold wind, I told myself. On one side of the headstone was written the inscription "Awarded the Purple Heart Feb. 1970," and on the other side, "Awarded the Bronze Star Feb. 1970."

I couldn't explain my thoughts and emotions as I stood looking down at the headstone. Thirty-two years had passed since I had been this close to Boyd. I was the last thing he ever saw as I knelt beside him on that small hill in Vietnam. He had looked into my eyes and tried to tell me something only to have his heart pump his lungs and mouth full of blood. I had watched helplessly as he died. I last saw him as I helped slide him into a black body bag and put him on a helicopter to start his long journey back to this place.

Next to his grave, a tombstone read "Geneva Wade, died 1993" and "Chester Wade," with a date of birth, but no death. His mother had died nine years before my visit to his grave, but his father was still alive. From the birth date of Boyd's father, my wife and I calculated that he was eighty-eight years old. As we had driven down the gravel road to the cemetery, we had passed a driveway with a sign above it bearing the words "Wade Ranch." I wondered if the people living there were a part of Boyd's family. I had no desire to bring back hurtful memories for anyone, but I felt a need to talk to his father, to explain that Boyd had not died alone, that he had many friends with him when he died. I stood at the grave for a long time in silence. *Good-bye, Boyd. It was an honor to have known you.*

I stopped at the house across from the ranch where an old man and woman were carrying sacks of groceries from their truck into the house. They greeted me, and I explained that I was looking for the family of Boyd Wade, that I had been with him when he was killed. They told me they were distant kin, but they knew Boyd's father and were sure he would like to meet me. They told me where he lived in town and urged me to see him. I asked my wife, Joyce, what she thought about my going to see Boyd's father. She said it was up to me. She knew it would be a hard thing to do, but she would understand whatever decision I made.

I drove up First Street, slowing down to look for 406. All too quickly we were sitting in front of the small, white wooden house. No vehicles were parked in the gravel drive. Joyce said she would stay in the car. I got out and slowly walked up to the front door. The main door was open, leaving only a glass storm door separating me from the living room, and what waited for me there. I knocked.

From inside came a voice, "Come in."

CHAPTER 1

Growing Up in Eastern Oklahoma

In 1956, I was seven years old, and I couldn't have been happier. My family lived on an eighty-acre farm in the forest-covered hills of eastern Oklahoma. Although I didn't know it at the time, the land wasn't good for farming. The acreage was situated on the north-facing slope of a large sandstone ridge. Over the eons, rain and wind had eroded most of the soil into nearby creeks and tributaries to be carried away and deposited in the Arkansas River's rich fertile delta valley. What remained was the poor, sandy, rocky soil that my father tried to farm with his antiquated horse-drawn equipment. Scrub oak and underbrush covered half the farm. On the other half he tried to raise peanuts, cotton, and sugarcane.

For me, it was the most delightful place on earth. I spent countless hours roaming through the thickets and brambles searching for targets for my slingshot, which I had made from the red rubber of an old tire tube. In the spring when my father plowed the fields with his team of horses, I followed behind, walking barefoot down the damp furrows of dirt and carrying an old rusty tin can to fill with worms for a fishing trip to the pond. My dog, Butch, a black-and-white beagle my mother despised for sleeping in her flowerbed, tagged along behind me. Whenever my father exposed a mole with his plow, I tossed the can of worms aside, and Butch and I chased it across the freshly turned earth.

My father was a quiet man. Born and raised less than a mile from our farm, his family had settled in eastern Oklahoma in the 1870s when the area was Indian Territory. Like many boys, he grew up helping his father on the family farm, and like many young men of his generation, he served his country in World War II. He had trained to invade Japan when America dropped the atomic bombs on Hiroshima and Nagasaki. Instead, he went there as part of the occupation forces.

When he came back to the States, he met my mother at a dance, and they were married a few months later. She was a tall, pretty brunette with a lively personality, the opposite of my father. While he was quiet and reserved, she was outgoing, forever with a smile on her face. She delighted in raising a large garden behind our simple four-room home built of rough sawn lumber. On the rare occasion when Butch and I chased down a cottontail rabbit and proudly carried it back to the house, she would smile at me and say, "Maybe he's not such a bad dog. At least that's one less rabbit that will eat my garden."

Sunday was my favorite day of the week. That was the day when we loaded up in our old car to visit my aunts and uncles. I was especially excited when we traveled down the three miles of bumpy, dusty dirt road that led to my uncle Olen's farm.

Uncle Olen and his family lived next to Emachaya Creek, a muddy little stream barely twenty feet wide. During periods of little rain it was reduced to mere pools of standing, moss-covered water. Uncle Olen had two boys about my age, and to us, Emachaya Creek was the Mississippi River. We would dig a large can of worms out from under my cousins' rabbit pens, grab cane poles, and head out to one of the pools of water to catch perch or mud catfish. When we grew tired of fishing, we turned rocks over in the shallow water, looking for crawdads, or battled up and down the creek banks in a mock war. As much fun as the fishing and playing were, I had another more important reason for wanting to go to Uncle Olen's farm.

One Sunday, as we stood in the creek skipping flat rocks across the long pool of water, I looked up the hill at my uncle's house and saw him, Aunt Sis, and my parents sitting on the back porch.

"Can we go now?" I asked one of my cousins.

He looked toward the house. "I guess, but we'll have to hurry or they'll catch us again," he said as we started up the hill. "We can pretend like we need a drink of water."

"Where are you boys going?" Aunt Sis asked as we opened the wooden screen door that led into the kitchen.

"We need a drink of water," I lied.

"Wipe your feet before you go in," she said, turning back to her conversation with my mother.

We walked past the wooden bucket of well water sitting on the kitchen cabinet and quietly made our way to the bedroom. I glanced at my uncle's guns hanging on a wall rack above the bed, but they weren't the reason we sneaked into his bedroom. We made our way to the dresser in the corner.

"Be careful and don't let it squeak when you open it," I whispered to my cousin. Once before, my aunt had heard the squeaky drawer and caught us.

He gently lifted the drawer and pulled it out. I stood on tiptoes to peer over the edge. Inside, beneath my uncle's neatly folded shirts, lay three leather-bound cases. My cousin reached in and lifted one of the cases.

"No, not that one," I whispered. "The one in the middle."

He placed the case back in the drawer and picked up the middle one. He gently opened the lid and handed the case to me.

The object I desired to see hung on a bright purple ribbon trimmed in white. The gold that lined the heart-shaped medal sparkled in the sunlight that shone through the bedroom window. I held the case for a long moment, staring at the golden image of the man in the heart's center. It was the most impressive sight a young boy could ever behold: the Purple Heart. I knew what it was and why my uncle Olen had it.

One day that summer he had come to our farm to help us gather our peanut crop. As we worked in the heat of the mid-afternoon sun, stacking peanuts around wooden poles to dry, my uncle pulled off his shirt. I worked nearby, and each time I met him at the pole with a load of peanuts, I stared at his chest. Finally, my curiosity got the best of me.

"What are those?" I asked, pointing to a row of round, deep, purple scars across his chest and shoulder.

He placed his finger on one of the purple indentations and grinned at me. "Ah, some German woman got mad at me during the war and shot me." He continued picking up peanut vines.

I worked a while longer and again met him at the pole. "Did it hurt?" I asked.

Again he grinned at me. "About like a yellow jacket sting," he said.

I wanted to ask more questions, but before I could say more, he said, "Ain't nothing for a little boy to worry about," and went back to work.

That night I asked my father how Uncle Olen had gotten shot. He told me Uncle Olen had been with a lot of soldiers in World War II at a place called Normandy Beach. Two days after they landed there, he was laying communication wire through the hedgerows when a female German soldier shot him several times with a machine gun. He spent many months in an army hospital and several years healing from the effects of his wounds.

When I asked my father what had happened to the German soldier, he said Uncle Olen's friends killed her. I wanted to know more, but he told me I was too young. "Wait until you are older," he said.

Aunt Sis called from the back porch, breaking my reverie. "What are you boys doing in there? I thought you wanted a drink of water."

We quickly replaced the medal in the drawer and gently pushed it closed. As we headed out the front door, Aunt Sis and my mother came in through the back. I heard Aunt Sis say something about sneaky boys.

When we returned to the creek, I tried talking my cousin into making up a different excuse to go back in the house for another look at the medal. My cousin mentioned the peach-tree switch his mother kept on the kitchen cabinet. I would have to wait several weeks for another Sunday visit before I could see the beautiful purple medal again.

When we resumed our play battles up and down the creek banks, my little boy's mind filled with images of daring feats and evil German soldiers. When my cousins yelled, "Bang, bang, bang, I got you," it didn't bother me. I had been stung by yellow jackets many times. It was a cheap price to pay to someday earn my own Purple Heart.

That summer of 1956 was our last spent on the farm. I started school that fall in Enterprise, at the same small country school my father had attended when he was a boy. Mrs. Lila, the only teacher, taught grades one through six in the same room, with a row of chairs for each grade. While she taught one grade at the front of the class, the others worked quietly at their desks and waited impatiently for recess. Mrs. Lila kept a paddling board on top of her desk for students who talked or raised their heads to look around the room.

I hated school. I cried each morning as I walked the one and a half miles across our neighbor's fields on my way to school.

In spite of my parents' best attempts at making a living on the farm, that winter they decided it was a failed effort. They were reluctant to sell and thought if they found work during the summer for a few years, they would be able to pay off the land and someday return to farming. We became a family of nomads, using the farm as a base for the winter months.

Each spring we journeyed to western Oklahoma to work in cotton and peanut fields. Oftentimes we remained there until late in the fall. We constantly moved from one town to the next to find work, and each time we moved, I started a new school. Between grades one through nine, I attended eleven different schools.

By 1961, my parents gave up holding on to the farm. To my sorrow, they sold it, and we moved to western Oklahoma so my dad could work for my uncle Willis, who owned a plumbing business. I didn't like the flat, arid countryside of the western part of the state. I missed the hilly, forest-covered terrain of eastern Oklahoma. I was relieved when, after my father obtained his plumbing license, we moved back to Quinton, a small town a few miles from our old farm.

Finally, I would get to spend the last three years of high school in one place. I had never had a close friend in school. By the time I learned the kids' names, we would have to move again. Everything changed when we moved to Quinton.

Dennis Guthrie, a skinny guy barely five feet six, was shooting hoops with a couple of boys in front of his house as I walked home after my first day of classes.

"Hey," he said to me. "Want to shoot some baskets with us?"

Our friendship began that day. We were like brothers. When our parents wanted to find us, all they had to do was call the other's house. Our mothers became so accustomed to our being together that when one of us showed up for dinner without the other, it was like a member of the family was missing.

When we got our driver's licenses, we dreamed of buying the hottest new muscle cars and dragging up and down the three blocks of our small town's main street. Dennis pined for a Pontiac GTO. My favorite was the Plymouth GTX. We spent countless hours figuring engine sizes, gear ratios, transmissions, colors, and other options for our dream cars.

Like millions of other kids who grew up then, we also were caught up in the "Sixties Revolution." The music we listened to, the emerging hippie culture, the drugs, and the changing attitudes about sexual behavior all combined to make our generation unique.

But in one respect our generation wasn't unique. Like most of the generations preceding us, we came of age as America was involved in a war. It wasn't a declared war like World War II, yet the news broadcasted daily accounts of what was going on in a little country in Southeast Asia called Vietnam. Dennis and I watched the newscasts about Vietnam with keen interest. We talked often about events there and even considered joining the army. When we were growing up, the men who had served in the military during the war years were regarded as heroes. Whether World War II or Korea was being discussed, we had never heard anyone say negative comments about the men who fought.

Dennis and I graduated from high school in 1967, and that summer we left for Arkansas to work on a large dam being constructed on the Arkansas River where his father was the construction superintendent. We decided to attend school that fall at a small junior college close to home. Dennis enrolled in civil engineering, and I took pre-pharmacy, but our college careers lasted one semester. I had spent my whole young life outdoors, and the thought of being cooped up in a building for the rest of my life didn't appeal to me. Dennis finally managed to buy his GTO, though he settled for a used car with a different color than he wanted. When his dream car became the source of much trouble between him and his parents, he quit school and joined the army.

In February of the following year, I married the girl I had been dating since high school and soon found myself facing the same problem my parents had struggled with for twenty years. Without a technical skill or a college degree, making a living in eastern Oklahoma was next to impossible. I considered returning to college, but the images of Vietnam on the nightly news haunted me. Dennis was likely headed there, and I reasoned that if I still wanted a college education in a few years, the army would pay for it when I returned. Besides, my thoughts on school hadn't changed since that first miserable day in Mrs. Lila's one-room country school back in Enterprise.

The army was the only choice that made sense to me.

CHAPTER 2

The Only Choice That Made Sense

I enlisted in the army in the spring of 1968. At last I would be a part of the organization I had heard so many stories about during my childhood. The trip to Fort Polk, Louisiana, was my first airplane ride. The small propeller-driven plane had no insulation to deaden the noise and offered only a bench with webbing behind for the other recruits and me to hold on to. We flew through a thunderstorm about halfway there, and the little plane popped and banged to the point that I was sure we were going to crash. Several of the new recruits flying with me got airsick and threw up at their feet. By the time we reached Fort Polk, I didn't care if I ever got on another airplane in my life.

The army recruiters I had talked to had been a mild-mannered, polite, accommodating group of people. They had addressed me by my first name when they answered all my questions concerning what life would be like for the next three years. The second group of people I met in the army, with stripes on their shoulders, also had called me by my first name. The funny thing is, somewhere along the way my name changed. Suddenly, instead of Gary, I was "Scumbag," "Shithead," "Numbnuts," or, if the drill instructors—DIs—felt good that day, simply "Recruit." From the moment I stepped off the olive drab bus at basic training, they had absolute control of my life.

Their objective was to strip us of our individuality and independence. We stood the way they wanted us to stand, we walked the way they wanted us to walk, and we went to the bathroom when they wanted us to go. Two minutes after we got off the bus, people were scattered everywhere doing push-ups, while others ran around and around the flagpole located in the center of the company area. When the drill instructors decided we had been sufficiently intimidated and humiliated, we were told to "fall in." On the asphalt in front of the barracks, some poor trainee had painted more than one hundred sets of footprints in bright yellow paint. Each of us found a set to stand on. The DIs told us to place our bags in front of us and stand at attention. Then they dumped the contents of each bag on the asphalt in front of the owner. Chewing gum, candy, books, transistor radios, and other contraband went into a large garbage can at the end of the formation. One unfortunate recruit had a condom hidden in his bag.

"And just what in the hell are you planning to do with this?" a DI screamed in his face. He held the condom in front of the trembling recruit's face, looking down the line at another DI, with just the hint of a grin on his face as if to say, "I've got one."

The other DI joined him.

"What are we going to do about this?" the first DI asked.

"Maybe we have a pervert here," the second replied.

"Why don't you go over there and hump that flagpole for a while," the first DI yelled.

All the time the rest of us were getting our bags pilfered, the poor guy was making love to a flagpole. For the remainder of basic, he was known as "Rubber." I learned one thing quickly—don't do anything stupid to attract the attention of the drill instructors.

The first day we also learned what all soldiers become proficient at in the army—standing in line and waiting. We stood in line to get our uniforms. The supply clerks looked over each of us to estimate size, which resulted in some ill-fitting uniforms. Next came boots.

They asked us what size we wore—a very important question for a recruit. Over the next eight weeks we would walk or run more than a thousand miles in those boots.

After the uniforms and other equipment were taken care of, haircuts and shots followed. Both were quick affairs. The barber didn't ask me how I wanted my hair. He started at the base of my neck and brought the two-inch-wide clippers over the top of my scalp to my forehead. The barber finished with a few more passes on the sides, taking twenty seconds at most. All hair was cut a uniform one-eighths of an inch long.

When the DIs told us it was time to get shots, I imagined nurses with syringes and needles. Instead, a group of privates stood holding futuristic-looking guns with long tubes attached. They warned us not to flinch. As we moved down the line, each in turn placed the gun to our arms and injected the serum under high pressure. Those who flinched or moved while receiving the injection were rewarded with blood running down their arms and another shot.

The DIs assigned us to our barracks, showed us how to fold a military corner on our bunk and arrange our footlocker, and gave us ten minutes to eat. Then we began our number one activity for the next eight weeks: physical training (PT). Learn-how-to-drill PT. Make-it-through-the-gas-chamber-and-be-nearly-choked-to-death PT. Go-to-a-first-aid-class-or-code-of-conduct PT. There was no end to the physical training, yet it produced the desired effect. The two-mile runs became easier and easier. Fifty push-ups were a breeze. After the initial shock of how we were treated by the drill instructors, I honestly began to enjoy parts of our training. I especially liked the rifle range. The M-14 was one of the best shooting rifles I had ever fired. On the day we qualified with it, I hit seventy-four out of the seventy-four targets.

One day halfway through our training, we stood in formation waiting for another company to clear the road. As I watched the other soldiers march by, I happened to see Dennis among them. I threw up my hand and waved at him. Instantly, the DI was in my face, screaming at me for not being at attention. The incident earned me two days of kitchen police duty under the supervision of the mess sergeant. Mess sergeants, I soon discovered, thrived on making recruits miserable.

As we neared the end of our training, the DIs mellowed to a degree. Sometimes they actually called us by our last names. One day I was summoned to the company headquarters by the platoon leader, a second lieutenant we seldom saw, as the DIs conducted most of our training. He told me that after reviewing my aptitude and proficiency scores I might want to consider applying for officer candidate school (OCS). He described the training, the pay, and the benefits of being an officer. He had graduated from OCS a few months earlier and told me that he didn't think I would have any problem making it through the training. I filled out the necessary forms and went back to work, not giving the matter much thought.

Late one evening, about a week before we were due to graduate from basic, Dennis walked into the barracks to see me. He had just finished advanced infantry training (AIT) at "Tigerland" across the base. He was on his way home for a few days' leave before reporting for duty to Vietnam. We had talked for only a few minutes when the DI walked in. Because Dennis was an unauthorized visitor, the DI went ballistic. We had no time for good-byes or see-you-laters. My last image of Dennis was of him being escorted out of the company area.

For the previous seven Saturdays, the other new recruits and I had heard the army band across the parade ground play its marching music for the trainees who finished basic. Finally, it was our turn. We stood in our starched khakis in the hot Louisiana sun and listened as some officer gave his weekly address. We were fine soldiers with our marksmanship badges pinned to our shirt pockets and our single stripes sewn to our sleeves. We didn't consider the fact that we had moved one step closer to our journey to Vietnam.

After graduating from basic training, I was ordered to the other side of Fort Polk to begin advanced infantry training. One morning, halfway through the unpleasant experience, the captain summoned me to company headquarters. He pushed a piece of paper across his desk and said, "Congratulations." It was a copy of the orders assigning me to Fort Benning, Georgia. I had been accepted into the officer candidate class of 6–69.

Fort Benning was an awe-inspiring place for a nineteen-year-old boy in 1968. On the bus ride to the Sixty-First Company where the other officer candidates and I would spend the next six months, we passed the United States Army Infantry School, a huge six-story building we would come to know well. To the southwest, clearly visible from our elevated company location, lay the Airborne School with its tall practice jump towers and large hangars where the parachutes were refolded after each jump. Any time of the day I could glance up into the sky and see the huge cargo planes in the distance spilling out their loads of men and equipment to float lazily back to earth under parachutes. It was quite an impressive sight for a young man from eastern Oklahoma.

If I thought basic training had been an experience in intimidation and psychological torment, it was like kindergarten compared to what awaited me during the first two months of OCS. In basic training, the DIs weren't trying to send us back home. Unless a recruit suffered a complete physical or mental breakdown, at the end of basic training he was declared a soldier and sent for advanced training. For the first two months of OCS, getting rid of us was exactly the instructors' objective. If a soldier failed an endurance or proficiency test, the company commander always had the option of putting him back in the enlisted ranks.

I was determined *not* to fail.

OCS was divided into three phases: basic, intermediate, and senior, each of two months' duration. Basic phase consisted primarily of a more intense version of basic training under the constant supervision of a platoon tactical (Tac) officer.

The other candidates and I were housed in multistory barracks with two men assigned to each room, which were much like college dorms. Each twelve-by-twelve-foot room was furnished with our own locker, bunk, and a desk and chair to sit in for hours while studying a continuous supply of handouts and books. A speck of dust or a slightly tarnished piece of brass would earn us demerits, as would an endless list of other infractions. Each demerit equaled an hour of marching from one end of a large parking lot to the other across from the barracks, with our movements monitored by an ever-vigilant Tac officer. A poorly executed about-face earned an extra demerit—a punishment reserved for weekends to occupy our spare time. For the first several months, the parking lot was full of officer candidates. I recall the distance across the parking lot as being exactly fifty-nine steps.

Each Friday we received a schedule for the coming week. For the first two months, one activity dominated our time: physical training. Unlike PT at basic training, PT at OCS could mean a variety of things. One time it might mean a three-mile run across the Chattahoochee River bridge, the next time an obstacle course designed and staffed by the Ranger Department. The black-beret–clad instructors inflicted as much pain as possible on the future second lieutenants, especially with their demonstrations on hand-to-hand combat and bayonet training with pugil sticks. We still had plenty of conventional PT to keep us busy, like doing the forty-yard low-crawl in twenty-three seconds while maintaining chest and hip contact with the ground at all times or running the mile in under six minutes while wearing combat boots. By the end of the first two months, several candidates who started the class had been dropped as unsatisfactory. A few had simply decided to quit.

The intermediate phase placed less emphasis on physical training and devoted more time to teaching us the knowledge we would need to become infantry officers. We still had enough contact with the Ranger PT sergeants to satisfy our need for physical activity, but we began to spend more and more time at the Infantry Hall and on the bleachers covering Fort Benning from one end to the other. Someone once said if you got lost on a night problem and worked your way to a hilltop without a set of bleachers on it, you were no longer on the Fort Benning Military Reservation.

We accumulated a stack of manuals and books that would have intimidated the most studious of college students. Instead of English 1113, our materials covered the deadly business of waging war. The M-16 rifle, the M-14 rifle, the M-60 machine gun, the .50 caliber machine gun, the 81 mm mortar, the light anti-tank weapon (LAW), the 90 mm recoilless rifle, and the 106 mm recoilless rifle were just a few of the subjects we spent hours learning at our desks and in the field. Not only did we learn to fire each type of weapon, we had to know details such as cyclic rate of fire, how to disassemble and reassemble, maximum effective range, and the killing radius of the shells fired. On each trip to the Infantry Hall we would be given books with titles such as *Map and Aerial Photograph Reading*, *Offensive Small-Unit Tactics*, *Map Reading*, and *Fundamentals of Defensive Combat Forward Rifle Platoon*. Our heads became full of numbers, arrows on a map, degrees and azimuths, deflections and elevations, call signs, directions, target identifications, and ranges. Each week we were tested on our accumulated knowledge, and those who failed to learn the information would be sent back to a class behind us or dropped.

The day we switched to senior phase, or "Blue Day," was a happy occasion, marking the first time in our short army careers that we would not be hazed and constantly harassed by a drill instructor or Tac officer. Each of us were even addressed by the Tac officers as "Senior Candidate." When we met one of the basic or intermediate candidates, he had to salute us the same as an officer.

A more intense regime of field exercises and studying followed the privileges. During the first few weeks of the senior phase, we spent a week in the field working on what was known as the "Ranger Problem." For five days and four nights, we trampled through the swamps and forests of southwest Georgia. We came to know the taste of water—purified by iodine tablets—from our canteens, the taste of a can of cold ham and lima beans from a C-ration meal, and the sweet sickening smell of army-issued bug repellant to fend off the hordes of mosquitoes that miraculously appeared at sundown in the Georgia swamps.

Under the nights' starry skies we were given a compass and map and told to find a marker some two or three thousand meters across the dark swamps and woodlands. If I and the other man on my team didn't return with the proper flag from our marker, we had to try the problem again. The only way to navigate in the dark was dead reckoning. We had to figure the azimuth and distance to our marker from the map. One of us held the compass on the proper heading and the other counted the steps as we moved. I was relieved when my partner told me that we had traveled the prescribed distance to our marker, and we found it a few meters off the side of our route.

On the nights we weren't tackling map problems, we set up defensive perimeters to guard against night attacks by aggressor forces— soldiers from other units who acted as Viet Cong. It was the only opportunity we got to rest while working on the assignment. Half the men stayed awake on guard duty while the other half tried to sleep on the hard, mostly wet Georgia ground.

By day we launched simulated attacks on the aggressors' villages. We put into practice all the small-unit tactics we had learned over the last several months. We spent hours preparing for one of these "operations." Logistics, equipment, routes, fire supports, and communication nets were planned under the watchful eye of our Ranger instructor. We were quite the sight with our camouflage paint and blank-firing adapters on the muzzles of our M-14s, charging up the slopes firing from the hip and yelling the things young men yell in such situations.

After completing the Ranger Problem, we went back to our barracks to finish our training. We all looked forward to the end of OCS, eager to get our commissions. A couple of weeks before graduation, I received the stunning news that Dennis was dead. He had been killed by a Viet Cong booby trap while serving with the Ninth Infantry Division in the Mekong Delta. Only a few days before the news of his death, I had received a C-ration box top from him. No note or letter, just a box top with his army post office address and mine at OCS. It was his way of seeing a little humor in my situation, being confined as I was to the strict regimen of training at OCS. I requested two days leave to attend his funeral. The commanding officer informed me that because he was not immediate family, I would be sent back to the next company behind us if I took off the two days. I would have to be content with my last image of Dennis at Fort Polk.

My classmates and I graduated on the fifteenth of February, 1969. I walked across the stage at the infantry school, and my wife pinned the gold bars on my collar. I was now a second lieutenant in the U.S. Army Reserve. We all celebrated our accomplishments. We didn't talk much about what we knew was soon to come.

After a short assignment to Fort Lewis, Washington, as a platoon leader in a basic training company, I received orders in the middle of August to report for duty to Vietnam. But the army had one more training step for me—two weeks of jungle training in the Panama Canal Zone.

Very little of the training I received in Panama related to the experiences I would encounter in Vietnam. I never found myself sleeping in a hammock at night, sliding down a rope across a river, or riding a landing craft in the ocean. Nonetheless, at the end of the two-week period, I was certified as a jungle expert. After a ten-day leave at home with my wife and family, I was ready to report to Vietnam.

CHAPTER 3

Assigned to Vietnam

Being assigned to Vietnam was a lonely experience. My father had often told me stories of his deployment to Japan with the occupation forces after the surrender. He had been a part of the same unit from training to final deployment. Such an experience allowed soldiers to face the challenges of a new assignment in an unfamiliar environment with people they knew. That wasn't the case for replacements sent to Vietnam. I boarded an airplane in Los Angeles, California, with a group of total strangers. The only thing we had in common was that we were headed to a strange and dangerous country halfway around the world.

It was uncommonly quiet aboard that flight. I suppose that, like me, each man was immersed in the thoughts of soldiers past, who—after all the training, the boasting to fellow soldiers of their future heroic deeds, and good-byes to their families and friends—realized that shortly they might face the ultimate enemy: death.

We stopped for refueling in Alaska. I had read many stories about the beautiful and cold far northern state, but my only memory of it today is the snowcapped mountains in the distance as we walked from the plane to the terminal. From Alaska we flew to Japan. I tried to sleep on the long flight, but each attempt at closing my eyes only made me more awake. Finally, I gave up and stared out the window at the endless ocean. Before it grew dark, I occasionally saw small, toy-like ships far below. I wondered where their voyages were taking them.

My only recollection of Japan is of a small gift shop in the terminal where a tiny old Japanese woman had a display of watches for sale. Her knowledge of English consisted of only two words—"hello" and "dollar"—which was better than my knowledge of her language. After several moments of sign language and me saying, "No, no, too much," I bought a watch with luminous dials for eighteen dollars. I figured it would quit before I got back on the plane, but it would work perfectly for the next year, despite the abuse it suffered from the monsoons, mud, and hard knocks of Vietnam.

Before long, we were back in the air, for the final leg. The captain's voice came over the intercom: "We are approaching the coast of Vietnam. Please fasten your seat belts." The stewardesses scurried around, gathering up the trays and cups from our meal. I strained to see my first glimpse of Vietnam out the window. It was not the picture I had imagined. I saw a land of swamps, canals, rivers, and rice paddies afloat on a sea of water. For several miles, the only dry land was the occasional clump of trees or a dike separating the myriad of fields. So this was what Dennis had meant in his letters when he spoke of constantly wading through water and never having dry feet.

We landed at Tan Son Nhut Air Base, near Saigon. As the plane rolled to a stop and the stairs were pushed up to the open door of the plane, a young specialist fourth class met the other replacements and me there and instructed us to go to a nearby building to collect our duffel bags. After collecting our bags, we were told to fall in and wait for the buses. We were in the middle of what appeared to be the busiest place on Earth, with the constant roar of fighter jets and helicopters taking off and landing and a continuous stream of trucks arriving and leaving the warehouses located around the base. It was like some choreographed, intricate dance.

A captain standing beside me pointed to a large group of olive drab–dressed men sitting on their duffel bags. "Those guys are going to get on that plane that just brought us here and go home," he said.

I didn't want to think about that. I had been in Vietnam thirty minutes, and trying to imagine a year passing and being in those guys' shoes was a little depressing. Across a large taxiway, a bright yellow forklift unloaded shiny metal caskets from the belly of a large cargo plane. Through the open door of the warehouse, we watched as the driver added each load to the neatly stacked and perfectly aligned rows. I was glad to see the buses arrive.

We boarded the buses and had barely begun to move when the bus I was riding sputtered to a stop. From the back, I could hear the driver uttering expletives as he tried in vain to get the bus restarted. After a few minutes, he slammed his open palms against the steering wheel, stood up, and told us to remain on the bus while he got the problem fixed. The driver flagged down a passing jeep and headed back toward the terminal. Sitting in a dark-colored bus in the middle of an air base with no shade in sight, we soon discovered just how hot the tropical sun could get. Despite our instructions to remain on the bus, the other passengers and I filed outside to seek the semi-cool relief of the shade the bus provided. In the distance, we could hear the boom of artillery pieces firing. Two hours later, a new bus arrived to take us to the Long Binh Replacement Center. It was a relief to get back on a bus and start moving. My sweat-soaked khaki uniform stuck to the vinyl on the back of my seat.

From the images I had seen on television, Saigon was a beautiful city with whitewashed buildings and palm-lined streets. There was no beauty to the Saigon I observed from the bus window. Mud and filth were everywhere. The smell of diesel fuel and human waste burning in barrels permeated the air.

The bus ride also provided me with my first opportunity to see the people of Vietnam. As we passed the sandbagged and barbed-wire checkpoints manned by the Army Republic of Vietnam (ARVN), I was struck by how small the Vietnamese soldiers were in their tight-fitting, tailored uniforms. They resembled boys of eight and ten years old, until I looked at their faces. The streets were packed with Vietnamese. Men pulling two-wheeled carts stacked with bags of rice or cords of firewood, women carrying baskets of fish or vegetables hanging from the ends of a split bamboo pole balanced on their shoulders, and the hordes of half-naked children all combined to make a strange sight to a young man from the United States. The feature that most surprised me was the expression on the faces of the people—a look of indifference sometimes blending into contempt for the American soldier. It was something I would never under-stand. Something I would come to hate about these people.

As we arrived at the Replacement Center, it was growing dark. I had not slept for forty-eight hours. I was thankful when a lieutenant showed the other newcomers and me the bachelor officers' quarters and mess hall and told us to report the next morning to headquar-ters for assignments. I didn't bother to go to the mess hall. I found a bunk and collapsed from the effects of jet lag and lack of sleep.

CHAPTER 4

Charlie Company's Taste of War

Five hundred kilometers to the north, a group of young Americans watched the sun come up. The men of Charlie Company stirred and stretched their legs after a long night in cramped foxholes hastily dug the night before on a steep mountain slope. Below them lay the 515 Valley, named for a forgotten road running through it. To the east, the first golden rays of the morning sun appeared over the South China Sea. It had been a restless night, as most in the jungle were. Contact with the North Vietnamese Army the day before occupied the men's thoughts. Shortly after establishing their night defensive position, or NDP, they had been mortared by the NVA. A grenade tossed at their position by an unseen enemy had wounded one soldier. The afternoon before, they had found an NVA soldier lying in the streambed they followed up the mountain. The NVA medics had attached a note to his uniform, indicating that he was suffering from jungle fever. They had told him to remain where he was. When the company interpreter read the note, it said his companions would return for him with a stretcher. The company hastily set up an ambush in the streambed, and shortly after, three NVA soldiers appeared to retrieve their sick comrade. One of the NVA men was killed, but the other two escaped up the mountain. This morning Charlie Company had orders to continue up the mountain.

By 0700 hours, the two ambush teams that had been sent out the night before closed on the company position. They reported negative contact. Lt. Robson Wills assembled First Platoon and prepared to move up the mountain. The platoon had been assigned to "walk point" for the company, at the front of the unit. At twenty-three years of age, Wills was considered the old man of the group by his platoon of nineteen- and twenty-year-olds. He had arrived in Vietnam in May, four months earlier.

Pvt. Kenneth Pease took the point, the first man in the front of the formation. Like most of the young men of the platoon, he was not called by his name, but rather by his nickname, Kentucky. The twenty-year-old from Hickory, Kentucky, had been in Vietnam for less than two months. Privates Nunes and Hernandez followed him. Sgt. Willard Wilson from Flint, Michigan, was close behind. He had been in the field with Charlie Company for less than thirty days.

Kentucky stared up the steep slope of the mountain. In places the only way he could make progress was to grab hold of roots and vines and pull himself up. The company had abandoned the streambed they used the day before. The NVA knew they were coming. After thirty minutes, the company commander called Lieutenant Wills, urging him to make better time up the mountain. Part of the company was still in the NDP.

In places the slope approached forty-five degrees. Several times, men would climb ten meters ahead only to slide back to their starting point. The sun was up, the heat increasing by the minute. Through openings in the jungle canopy, Lieutenant Wills could see two Cobra helicopter gunships and a small observation helicopter working the area just south of Landing Zone (LZ) "Liz." They would soon be in need of the Warlord team (the radio call sign for the helicopters).

Above Charlie Company, the NVA commander issued orders for the withdrawal of more than one hundred soldiers under his command. He was kept constantly aware of Charlie Company's position by the scouts and lookouts posted above their route up the mountain. Eight hundred meters northwest of where Charlie Company would reach the crest of the mountain ridge lay the base camp his unit had used for some time. His soldiers had constructed more than a dozen large hooches under the jungle canopy and had even carried cement at night from the valley below to build concrete bunkers. While most of his men carted the heavy weapons and supplies deeper into the mountains, he planned a delaying action to make the Americans pay for forcing him to abandon his comfortable base camp.

He knew he could not fight the soldiers climbing the mountain for longer than an hour. By then they would have all their supporting firepower at hand. He called one of his platoons forward and broke it down into four groups. If the Americans continued their present course up the mountain, they would emerge amid a large outcropping of rocks near the crest of the ridge. He carefully placed his men in a U-shaped ambush with two positions facing the crest and a position on each of the flanks. Each position would withdraw and escape along a different route when the ambush was over. But he needed the Americans to continue their present course up the mountain.

They did.

Kentucky moved cautiously ahead. The ground had leveled out somewhat, and the going was easier. Ahead, through heavy brush, he could see a large black rock as big as one of the Vietnamese hooches in the valley below. To the side lay more rocks, some large and others smaller. He looked back at the men behind him and signaled that he would move around the large rock and check out the area ahead. Nunes and Hernandez watched as he disappeared around the rock. A single shot rang out, followed by complete silence. The men looked at each other for a long moment. They called out, "Kentucky, Kentucky." No answer. They dropped their packs and started crawling through the rocks. When they reached the other side, machine gun and AK fire ripped the ground around them. Bullets ricocheted off the rocks overhead. Grenades exploded in front of their position.

They returned fire, quickly expending magazine after magazine toward the enemy positions. Lieutenant Wills moved another squad forward and followed it to a position near Nunes and Hernandez. At 0910, Charlie Company radioed battalion that its lead element was under heavy enemy fire. The Warlord team working south of Liz was immediately dispatched to the company's location. The rest of the company struggled to reach the crest of the ridge. Sergeant Wilson tried to move to a location where he could fire at one of the NVA positions. He went down, dead. Several others were wounded. When the Warlord team arrived overhead at 0930 hours, it reported to battalion headquarters that it was taking fire and that Charlie Company was in a horseshoe-type ambush.

Nunes looked behind him and saw Kentucky sitting on the ground, leaning against a rock as if he were resting. He had blood on his neck and shoulder. Nunes and Hernandez crawled to Kentucky's position. When they reached him, Hernandez grabbed Kentucky's shoulder and shook him, calling out, "Kentucky, Kentucky." As he shook Kentucky, the point man's head rolled off his shoulders, held by a single piece of skin. Hernandez freaked out. He continued to shake him.

Nunes called out to Hernandez, "He's dead, he's dead. He's dead, there is nothing we can do for him." Nunes got Kentucky's ammunition bandoleer and crawled back to his position in the rocks. He fired toward the NVA when his M-16 jammed.

Lieutenant Wills, who was near Nunes, heard him stop firing and raised his head over a rock to check on him. He looked at Nunes and said, "Nunes, are you—"

As Nunes looked up at the lieutenant, a bullet smashed through Wills's head.

By 1015 hours it was over. The NVA soldiers withdrew through the heavy cover to rejoin their unit deep in the mountains to the northwest. There was little danger of the Americans pursuing them. The ambush worked just as the NVA had planned. Air strikes and artillery barrages followed, but the odds of hitting the NVA in the vast expanse of the jungle and mountains were small. Behind them lay three dead American soldiers and five wounded. Charlie Company called for an urgent Dust Off—the call sign for aeromedical evacuation—for its wounded men. Because of the overhead canopy, the men had to be extracted by slings, which took forty-five minutes. The Dust Off pilot refused to take out the dead with slings. Charlie Company would have to carry them several hundred meters to a small clearing. An hour later the Warlord team found the abandoned NVA base camp and destroyed it with rockets.

Charlie Company moved east and established a defensive perimeter on the side of the mountain. The mood of the company was somber. At 1440 hours the soldiers reported to battalion that the enemy prisoner of war they had captured in the streambed the day before had died in the exchange of gunfire with the NVA that morning.

For many of the young men of Charlie Company, that encounter with the enemy had been their first taste of real war. For me, the events of that morning held a different significance. With the death of Lieutenant Wills, First Platoon, Charlie Company no longer had a platoon leader. The C-130 that eventually brought me to LZ "Bronco" would land a few hundred meters from where he lay in a black plastic body bag.

CHAPTER 5

The My Lai Massacre

I've got to go meet God—and explain all those men I killed . . .
Field Marshall Montgomery, 1976

As I collapsed on my bunk in the bachelor officers' quarters that first day in Vietnam, I had no idea what the future would hold over the course of the next year. Like the members of Charlie Company, ambushed on the mountainside, I would come to know that war means killing and dying.

Sometimes killing is simply killing. It is an easy thing to do when you have been properly trained and handed the weapon on the battlefield. For an instant you think of the person in your sights as only a silhouette target back on the noisy firing range at Fort Polk. You are elated to see him stumble and fall at the report of your rifle. It is only after the firing stops and the field becomes eerily quiet that you walk up to this target and realize you have just killed. You don't think of the possibility that it could have been you lying there with open, unseeing eyes and body torn apart. You are too young to think such thoughts. You are fascinated by the power you hold in your hands. It will be an easy thing to return home if you survive this war, which you surely will, and to forget the things you have done in this place.

You have made the man flying overhead very happy. You have added one more to his body count.

If having a high body count—or the proper kill ratio of U.S. soldiers dead to the number of enemies killed—was the measure of success or failure in Vietnam, the rifle platoon I would find out I was to lead, one of three making up Charlie Company, probably held the distinction of having the most kills of any to operate there. The problem with that statistic is most of those killings occurred on the morning of March 16, 1968, a year and a half before I arrived, in a small hamlet in Quang Ngai province called My Lai 4.

One of four companies that made up First Battalion, Twentieth Infantry, Charlie Company traced its proud heritage back to the American Civil War, when the unit had served under the command of Gen. George Sykes. Thereafter known as "Sykes' Regulars," the regiment had fought in nearly all of America's military campaigns from Second Bull Run and Gettysburg to the Battle of the Little Bighorn, World War I, World War II, and Korea.

In Vietnam for barely three months, Charlie Company and the rest of the battalion were part of the Eleventh Light Infantry Brigade, one of three brigades that made up the Americal Division headquartered at Chu Lai in I Corps in northern South Vietnam.

Charlie Company's normal area of operations (AO) there was around Landing Zones Bronco and Liz, which were located near Duc Pho on Highway 1 some forty kilometers to the south of My Lai, a village made up four hamlets designated by numbers. In the few months the company had operated around Bronco and Liz, the soldiers had failed to make substantial contact with the Viet Cong or North Vietnamese Army. In late January of 1968, Charlie Company received orders to join a special task force being created to cover an area left vacant by the withdrawal of the U.S. Marines and a South Korean marine brigade around and east of Quang Ngai City to the north. The task force consisted of three rifle companies from the Eleventh Brigade. Charlie Company, First Battalion, Twentieth

Infantry; Alpha Company, Third Battalion, First Infantry; and Bravo
Company, Fourth Battalion, Third Infantry became Task Force
Barker, named after its commander, Lt. Col. Frank Barker.

The South Vietnamese government and U.S. commanders considered the area the task force moved into to be one of the Viet
Cong's most tightly controlled territories, a reputation dating back
to the time of the French occupation. During their war with the
French, the Viet Minh had considered the area to be a "liberated
zone" and had even established a small arms factory there. Charlie
Company and the other companies soon discovered how well the
area deserved its reputation. They began to take casualties from
snipers, mines, and booby traps.

In mid-February, a combined operation in the area of My Lai over
a three-day period resulted in the deaths of five Americans and the
wounding of more than a dozen. An enemy body count of more
than seventy-five was reported for the operation, although not one
enemy weapon was captured. On February 23, the task force conducted another combined operation in the vicinity of My Lai 4 based
on intelligence that a Viet Cong battalion used the area as a base for
operations and supplies. As one of the companies began moving in
on its objective, the soldiers came under heavy fire from machine
guns, mortars, and small arms in the vicinity of the village of My Lai
4. After several hours of intense fighting, which included air strikes
and helicopter gunship fire, the Viet Cong withdrew and disappeared among the civilian population or hid underground in the
maze of tunnels that ran throughout the area. Although the Americans again reported a large body count, they had captured few
weapons and sustained one casualty, with more than a dozen
wounded. A predictable pattern emerged. Each time the task force
went near the villages of My Lai, it made contact with the enemy or
lost men to mines or booby traps.

On March 15, 1968, the new Eleventh Brigade commander,
Col. Oran Henderson, flew to Task Force Barker's headquarters at

Landing Zone "Dottie" and urged Lieutenant Colonel Barker to destroy the Viet Cong battalion thought to be operating around My Lai. That afternoon, Barker assembled his three company commanders, and he and his staff briefed them on an operation to be carried out the next morning. The operation would begin at 0725 hours with an artillery barrage, after which Charlie Company would "combat assault" its way into a landing zone immediately west of My Lai 4 and then sweep east through the village. Bravo Company would reinforce Charlie Company if needed or conduct its own combat assault east of My Lai 4 into an area known as "Pinkville" (so called because of its color on the companies' tactical maps). Alpha Company would move from its present field location to a blocking position north of My Lai to cut off the Viet Cong's escape. Barker and his company commanders hoped this operation would finally trap the Viet Cong battalion.

Before dawn, First Platoon, Charlie Company—led by Lt. William Calley—gathered on the pickup site at LZ Dottie. This would be the company members' first large-scale combat assault on a suspected enemy position—and a chance to get even for the loss of their friends and fellow soldiers over the last several weeks. In the briefing they received the night before from their company commander, Capt. Ernest Medina, the captain led them to believe the 48th Viet Cong local force battalion would be located in and around the village of My Lai 4. Their mission was to kill the enemy and destroy the village. They were told to shoot the livestock, destroy all foodstuffs, pollute the wells, and burn the village. They were told the residents of My Lai were Viet Cong or Viet Cong supporters and the few civilians who lived there would be gone to market or working in the fields by the time they arrived. In reality, the village would be occupied by hundreds of old men, women, and children.

To the south, in the dimly lit sky of dawn, the men of Charlie Company could barely see the long line of helicopters arriving from LZ Bronco. They would carry First Platoon and the rest of Charlie

Company to the hamlet of My Lai 4 where the company would add another chapter to the legacy of Sykes' Regulars. The men of Charlie Company loaded their weapons. Some fixed bayonets to the muzzles of their M-16s.

The smell of wood smoke from cooking fires permeated the air in the hamlet of My Lai 4. Children laughed and played in front of their straw-roof homes while their mothers and grandmothers prepared the morning meal of rice and fish in blackened pots hanging over open fires. A gentle breeze drifted in from the east off the South China Sea, swaying the leaves of the bamboo and banana trees, which would provide welcome shade during the afternoon's oppressive heat. For now, the breeze was cool and fresh. The sun's early morning rays were just beginning to filter into the courtyards and open squares of the village.

For nearly an hour, the villagers had been up preparing for their daily routine of gathering firewood, tending livestock, mending rice paddy dikes, and drawing water from the communal wells for drinking, bathing, and laundry. Theirs was a way of life that had existed for countless generations. No one in the village knew when the little hamlet had first been settled. They had no written record, only the stories handed down from one generation to the next. In a small corner of each of their homes, each family kept a shrine honoring their ancestors. They were content to live their lives as the old people of their families had lived before them.

Aside from the rare visit by a heavily guarded South Vietnamese provincial official, or frequent visits by Viet Cong committee members trying to recruit young men or to obtain food supplies, the villagers largely ignored the war going on around them. They didn't care who won. They wanted to be left alone to raise their families in this village where they had been raised. They were unaware that, a few miles to the north, young American soldiers wheeled their massive artillery guns around and pointed them in the direction of their home.

Already that morning many of the men and their wives had left the village, leaving small children in the care of their grandparents. Some traveled to the river east of the village to check fishing nets, while others started the six-mile walk to the markets in Quang Ngai City. Behind them they heard the deep rumbling of explosions, which lasted for several minutes. Barely visible to the northeast, a double row of helicopters appeared to be landing near their home. If the Americans did land there, surely they would only ask their usual questions about the whereabouts of the VC, pick up a few of the young men for questioning, and move on. That was what they always did.

At the first sound of the thunderous explosions on the west side of the village, the old men and women within it grabbed the children and ran for the protection of the family bomb shelters. A few Viet Cong who had spent the night in the village grabbed their rifles and ran toward the surrounding countryside.

The operation began as planned. Lieutenant Calley's platoon was on the first flight of "Dolphins," the call sign for the UH-1D helicopters, bringing half the company to the landing zone. As the helicopters approached the LZ, smoke from the more than a hundred rounds of 105 mm artillery shells fired to "soften up" the LZ began to drift away on the morning breeze. Although aimed at the LZ, some of the highly explosive rounds landed on the western edge of the village, destroying several of the villagers' homes. As the helicopters touched down, the American soldiers could see and hear the helicopter gunships placing machine gun and rocket fire on the tree line along the edge of the village. One of the small scout helicopters accompanying the operation reported seeing several armed Viet Cong, clad in black pajamas, fleeing from the village. As the Americans secured the LZ and waited for the remainder of Charlie Company to arrive on the second lift of choppers, several Viet Cong suspects were sighted in the fields surrounding the LZ. They were quickly cut down by rifle and machine gun fire. None of them had been armed.

When the last flight of Dolphins delivered the remainder of Charlie Company to the LZ, Captain Medina ordered Lieutenant Calley to get his platoon on line and to sweep through the southern half of the village. Second Platoon would sweep through the northern half. Third Platoon and Captain Medina with his radio-telephone operator (RTO) and staff remained at the LZ to coordinate the operation.

Despite all the predictions made by the operation's planners concerning the presence of the 48th Viet Cong unit, the LZ had been "cold." No one fired a single shot at Charlie Company. First and Second Platoon started across the clearing in a long, straight line from south to north, firing from the hip—a classic infantry tactic designed to suppress an enemy's fire while approaching his position. The Americans had practiced the tactic often back on the firing ranges in the United States and Hawaii where they trained before coming to Vietnam. The use of this tactic sent a message to the young men of Charlie Company that morning in March of 1968: shoot anything that moves in front of you. As they entered the edge of the village, the killing began. What followed between the hours of 0800 and 1030 that morning would become known as the "My Lai massacre."

Over the next two and a half hours, what happened at My Lai was largely determined by the individual morals of each soldier. When the long line of soldiers entered the village, all command of and control over them was lost, except for among the few who remained in sight of the platoon leaders and squad leaders. The men broke up into small groups, roaming through the village and shooting everything that moved. Although there were no direct orders to kill civilians, many of the soldiers interpreted the previous night's briefing to mean just that—to destroy the village and everyone in it. All around the village came the sound of gunfire and explosions as the soldiers shot men, women, children, and the villagers' animals. Some of the men refused to participate in the killings. A few became so sickened by what was happening around them that they became physically ill and vomited. Some of the more compassionate groups of men gathered up the villagers and took them to a place of safety away from the burning and shooting. Members of First Platoon took eighty-some Vietnamese to a large drainage ditch east of the village. They rounded up another group of about fifty and took them to a trail on the south side.

The Vietnamese villagers rounded up by First Platoon squatted alongside the drainage ditch. Mothers held infants in their arms and tried to quiet their other young children standing beside them. Old women wailed and sobbed after watching the Americans shoot down their families back in the village. They didn't understand the American soldiers' behavior. Twice before they had come to the village, and both times the soldiers had passed out food and candy and their medics had treated the sick.

Nearby, Lieutenant Calley talked on the radio to Captain Medina, who demanded to know what was slowing their sweep through the village. When Calley told the captain they had been delayed by gathering a large group of civilians, Captain Medina's reply was to the effect of get rid of them. Calley interpreted this instruction to mean "execute them." He ordered some of his men to help him and began pushing and throwing the villagers into the ditch. They fired their weapons down into the ditch, stopping occasionally to change magazines in their rifles. When the firing stopped, there was no movement from the bottom; body parts lay scattered around the sides of the embankment. The soldiers moved to the second group of villagers on the trail. Their fate was the same.

While First Platoon swept through the southern half of My Lai 4, Second Platoon also went on a killing spree in the northern section and in another small village a few hundred meters to the north. They killed between sixty and seventy Vietnamese men, women, and children. Third Platoon, along with Captain Medina and the company command group, remained at the LZ monitoring the operation. By 0830 hours that morning, the official body count by Charlie Company, relayed back to the brigade headquarters by Captain

Medina, had reached ninety. He also reported that they had recovered two weapons. When he and Third Platoon followed First and Second Platoon through the village, they burned what few houses remained and killed twelve women and children.

By 10:30 A.M. when headquarters gave the final order to cease fire, most of the inhabitants of My Lai 4 lay dead in large groups or scattered throughout the village where they had been dragged from their homes or bunkers. Many who had refused to come out of their bunkers were killed when soldiers tossed hand grenades inside. The only injury Charlie Company suffered was a soldier who accidentally shot himself in the foot with a .45 caliber pistol.

Bravo Company, operating east of My Lai 4 nearly two kilometers away, reported thirty-eight Viet Cong killed, none of whom were reported as women and children. The company suffered one casualty, or U.S. killed in action (KIA), and had seven soldiers wounded in action (WIA), from booby traps.

My Lai was a regrettable tragedy in U.S. military history, as were the deaths of nearly fifty-eight thousand American soldiers and close to three million Vietnamese during the war. The actual number of Vietnamese killed that day will never be known with certainty. The U.S. Army Criminal Investigations Division estimated the number at more than four hundred. Viet Cong propaganda indicated that U.S. forces had killed more than five hundred people in and around My Lai.

For the American soldiers who participated in My Lai and survived to return home, the images of the massacre were left etched in their minds. What they did and the events they witnessed will stay with them until they draw their last breath. But these are not the only images that remain from that morning. Ron Haeberle, a photographer for the Eleventh Brigade, had been assigned to photograph the operation by the Public Information Department back at brigade headquarters. In addition to taking black-and-white photographs with his army-issued camera, he took several color pictures with his personal camera. When these pictures were published in the United States, America was horrified. The grizzly scenes of dead women and children piled along a dirt path, pictures of young American soldiers burning these dead people's homes, and finally the picture of an executed woman lying on the ground with her brain spilling out from under the edge of her straw hat brought the reality of what had happened to the American people.

As horrific as these few photographs are, they pale in comparison to the images that were etched in the minds of the young men who committed the acts. To watch as a bullet you fired strikes another human being and takes away his or her life forever changes you. The things you see and do in such situations become a permanent part of your life.

For me, these kinds of images, along with the sounds and smells, and the feelings they produced, would begin on the September day in 1969 when I arrived at LZ Bronco to join Charlie Company as a twenty-year-old second lieutenant. The news of what had happened at My Lai and the subsequent cover-up was just beginning to unfold in the American press. Most of the men of Charlie Company who participated in the killings at My Lai had completed their tours and returned to the United States. The few who extended their tour or volunteered for another were being picked up by the U.S. Army's Criminal Investigation Division to give statements or serve as witnesses in future courts-martial.

When I was assigned to lead First Platoon, which had been Lieutenant Calley's platoon, the brigade commander told me our mission was to kill the enemy and win the hearts and minds of the Vietnamese people. Winning hearts and minds would prove a difficult task with the unit that had slaughtered close to five hundred people a few miles away. Although my men and I had had nothing to do with the killings, we would experience the consequences of them. Undoubtedly, many of the farmers and villagers in the area

where we operated had known or been related to some of the people killed at My Lai.

While the army had been successful for more than a year in keeping the events of that March morning from the American people, it
had no such control over the spread of information among the Viet
Cong and the Vietnamese people. Charlie Company and the rest of
Task Force Barker had given the Viet Cong propaganda teams a valuable counter argument to any attempts we made to convince the
people we were trying to help them. When we would go into a village
to provide security for a medical team there to treat their sick, most
often we would be greeted by looks of mistrust and hostility. I
learned from our company interpreter that following such visits, the
Viet Cong would come that night, or soon afterward, and explain to
the villagers that the Americans had also treated the sick of My Lai.
Then they would read the names of the women and children who
had been killed by the Americans. From the interpreter I also
learned of rumors that the Viet Cong had placed a monetary bounty
on the head of any member of Charlie Company killed.

At first it was difficult for me to understand these things, but as I
watched what people were capable of doing to each other in the
name of war, how the deaths of a few young boys seemed so insignif-
icant to the people in charge, I came close to understanding how the
brutality and savagery buried deep within each of us might be
unleashed.

CHAPTER 6

Taking Command

The next morning I woke at dawn. I put on my sweat-soaked, wrinkled khakis and went outside to watch the sun rise. Overnight in Saigon, it had rained, and the morning breeze felt cool compared to the previous day's heat. I was soon to learn that the morning coolness didn't last. By the time the sun was thirty minutes into the sky, the temperature had climbed dramatically. After a breakfast of powdered eggs and stale link sausage, I began the tedious process of checking into Vietnam. I moved from one unpainted wooden building to the next, filling out forms. Finance forms, insurance forms, and notification forms. After several hours, a clerk handed me a folder containing a copy of all the forms I had filled out and a copy of my orders and boarding pass. I was told to report to the transportation area and to catch a bus back to Tan Son Nhut at 1400 hours. I had a couple of hours to kill, so I went back to the bachelor officers' quarters, where a large map of Vietnam hung. My orders said American Division at Chu Lai. I searched the map and finally found Chu Lai at the northern end of South Vietnam, located close to the South China Sea in I Corps. A captain came through the door and walked over to the map.

"Where are they sending you?" he asked.

"American Division at Chu Lai," I replied.

"Damn," he said under his breath.

He left me there, staring at the map and wondering what he'd meant by "damn."

I caught the bus back to Tan Son Nhut, the ride just as hot as the day before. I checked in at the flight desk and showed a sergeant my boarding pass.

"That's your flight right over there, lieutenant," he said, pointing to a C-130 with its cargo door lowered to the ground.

I went over to the cargo plane and showed my pass to the load-master who told me to find a place to sit. The cargo area was full of crates containing C rations, ammunition, and many other contain-ers stamped "U.S. Army." I found a place to sit on an aluminum bench near the rear door. The accommodations were much differ-ent than on the Pan Am flight the day before.

The trip north provided my first good look at the country where I would spend the next year of my life. We flew with the cargo door half open so I could see out the rear of the plane as we traveled up the coast, just offshore. The white sandy beaches stood in sharp con-trast to the lush green vegetation on the coastal plain. Nearly every flat piece of ground had rice paddies. With their nonsymmetrical layout of dikes, the paddies formed a green maze of lines when viewed from the air. I soon discovered they weren't so beautiful when you had to wade through them.

While I noticed the beauty of the white sand beaches and the sun reflecting off the water of the rice paddies, what most grabbed my attention were the ominous, dark, blue-green mountains that kept advancing on and receding from the coast as we flew northward. At times they extended all the way to the shore and then they would retreat back several kilometers. After growing up in the hilly, forested area of eastern Oklahoma and spending some time in the dense forests of northern California, I was accustomed to the lack of visibility in the woods. But nothing I had ever experienced would compare to the first time I stepped into the tree line of those moun-tains. They would become a place of fear.

From the relative safety of the C-130, the countryside looked deceptively peaceful. The only evidence of warfare was the occasional shell crater visible in one of the rice paddies below.

As we flew up the coast, the plane suddenly made an abrupt 180 degree turn and lost about one thousand feet of altitude on a steep decent toward a runway and complex of buildings below. I glanced at the loadmaster sitting beside me half dozing and asked what the hell that was all about.

He looked at me and replied, "We don't spend much time circling around the mountains. You might get a heavy-caliber machine gun round up your ass."

The war was getting closer.

After we landed, I reported to another processing center. The American Division conducted a weeklong orientation class for all the replacements. Officers were exempt, so I had to wait a couple of days to find out to which of the brigades I would be assigned. The processing center was located next to the beach. After classes dismissed in the late afternoon, soldiers would scrounge air mattresses and planks of wood and swim and surf along the shore. My first day there, a young private paddled out into the surf on an air mattress. By the time the young men swimming with him noticed that he had disappeared beneath the waves, it was too late. He was dead. A helicopter was called in, and it took his body to graves registration—the military's center for processing bodies and shipping them home. I couldn't help thinking that four days earlier his parents, and perhaps his wife, had kissed him good-bye and watched as he flew off to war. "Nonhostile casualty accident" was the army's term for the young man's death.

The next morning my name was on a list posted on the bulletin board at the personnel office. I had another unit assignment. I was headed southward to the Eleventh Light Infantry Brigade, headquartered at Duc Pho. After waiting a couple of hours, I caught a flight on another C-130 about to make a supply run there. Another plane ride, only this one was much shorter. Had I known where to look, I would have been able to see the deserted village of My Lai 4 as we passed over it.

After a few minutes, the C-130 banked inland four kilometers and landed near the Eleventh Brigade headquarters. A large sign read "11th Infantry Brigade Welcomes You to LZ Bronco, Home of the Americals Jungle Warriors." Bronco lay just to the east of National Interprovincial Highway 1, better known on our maps as Q.L. 1. The local GI name for it was "The Red Ball." It was the only road that ran from one end of Vietnam to the other. Between Bronco and the highway, and on either side of Q.L. 1, lay the small Vietnamese village of Duc Pho. In addition to being the headquarters for the Eleventh Brigade, LZ Bronco also served as the rear headquarters and supply storage area for the battalions that comprised the brigade. After a brief meeting with the brigade commander, the personnel officer, or S-1, informed me that I was assigned to the First Battalion, Twentieth Infantry. A jeep and driver took me around to the other side of Nui Dang (Dang Mountain), to the battalion's headquarters area.

The driver took me to the First of the Twentieth's compound, where I found out that I had been assigned to Charlie Company. I made my way to the company headquarters building and met the company first sergeant, otherwise known as "Top," one of the most likeable men I ever met in the army. He had the clerks fill out the usual forms and told me that a supply chopper would be leaving for "Liz" in a couple of hours. He walked over to supply with me and helped me draw my field equipment and an M-14 rifle with a six-power scope on it. I didn't like the unreliable M-16 and had already made up my mind to carry the M-14 if possible. The M-16 I had trained with back at Fort Polk in AIT had constantly malfunctioned. Ammunition for the M-14 would be no problem, as it fired the same bullet as the M-60 machine gun.

As we walked back to the headquarters building, Top said, "Lieutenant Bray, if you don't mind, I'd like to give you a little advice."

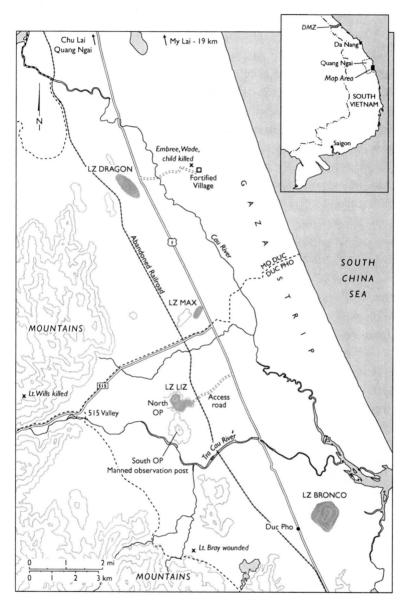

Charlie Company's Area of Operations, 1969–1970

"Sure, go ahead, Top," I said.

"Listen to the guys out there who have been around for a while. Even if it's from a PFC (private first class). Sometimes what they tell you might save someone's life. If you make it through the first couple of months, your chances of getting through this goes up a lot. You have a great CO (commanding officer) who cares a lot about his men and tries his best to take care of them."

"Thanks, Top." I could tell from his voice that he was being sincere. We went back to HQ, and he showed me a footlocker where I could stow my personal belongings. I put away my khaki uniform and copies of all the paper forms I had accumulated over the last several days. As I tucked items into my backpack, he looked at me and grinned.

"Remember, sir, you'll have to carry every ounce of that stuff with you in the field."

When I was finished, I picked up the pack. It didn't feel too heavy to me. Within a week, I sent most of it back for him to put in storage.

The helicopter landed at the battalion supply depot with a loud whoop-whoop-whoop of its rotors. I climbed in and sat on the metal seat facing the side to look out the open door. The flight to LZ Liz would be a short one, as it was only six kilometers away. As the helicopter climbed into the sky and flew around the north side of Bronco, I saw rows of helicopters parked in huge earthen revetments. Other revetments were packed full of artillery ammunition. On the nose of some of the helicopter gunships were painted large teeth. I would come to know these gunships well over the next year. They were from the 174th Assault Helicopter Company. The choppers' radio call sign was "Shark." With their mini-guns and rockets blazing, they were a welcome sight overhead whenever we got into a tight spot. I never saw them back away from anything.

As the supply helicopter gained altitude, I got my first good look at the terrain where the First Battalion operated. Over the next year I would walk virtually every square meter of it. Highway 1 ran north-

northwest from LZ Bronco, parallel to the coast of the South China Sea, toward Quang Ngai City and Chu Lai. The roughly four-kilometer-wide strip of land between Q.L. 1 and the sea was known as "the Gaza Strip." It was a mixture of swamps, rice paddies, streams, sand dunes, thick stands of bamboo, saltwater evergreen brush, and villages. In other words, the perfect operating area for the Viet Cong. I would spend nearly half my year patrolling up and down this booby-trap–infested strip of land. Approximately two kilometers west of Q.L. 1 and running parallel to it was an abandoned railroad bed. The Viet Cong had long since destroyed all the bridges, and the Vietnamese people had used the railroad iron and cross ties to construct bunkers. All that remained now was the elevated berm. Vietnamese villages heavily populated the area between the berm and Q.L. 1. West of the abandoned railroad lay the 515 Valley, named for an overgrown and unused road running from Q.L. 1 back into the mountains. The 515 Valley was roughly triangular shaped, with its twelve-kilometer base running along the railroad bed. The apex of the triangle extended approximately six kilometers west to the base of the mountains. Near the apex of this triangle, the Song Tra Cau (River Tra Cau) exited the mountains and flowed eastward to the South China Sea. West of 515 Valley and forming both sides of the triangle were the jungle-covered mountains, which rose quickly to an elevation of more than six hundred meters. When operating in 515 Valley, it didn't take much to imagine the NVA and Viet Cong hidden on the steep slopes of the mountains, constantly watching you.

The helicopter approached LZ Liz, which was situated two kilometers west of the Red Ball between Xuong Rong and Xuong Giong mountains, better known to the GIs as the North OP (observation post) and South OP. LZ Liz sat almost directly in the middle of 515 Valley. Roughly rectangular in shape, the landing zone covered an area nearly three hundred meters north to south, and five hundred meters east to west. A single-lane paved access road led from LZ Liz east to Q.L. 1. Large sandbag bunkers, located at strategic points around the perimeter, surrounded Liz. A hill made of sandbags—that was my first impression flying overhead. Liz would be my home, a place of relative security during the next year.

The battalion operating procedure was for three of its companies to be in the field conducting operations while the fourth company provided security for LZ Liz. The rotation was based on a weekly cycle; each company spent three weeks in the field and one week providing security. When I landed on Liz, Charlie Company had just returned from the operation in the mountains to the west, where Lieutenant Wills had been killed, to begin its week of security duty.

The helicopter touched down next to the battalion command post. Beside the landing zone was another sign, reading, "Welcome to LZ Liz, Home of the 1st Battalion, 20th Infantry—'Sykes' Regulars'" beneath two pairs of crossed rifles.

I walked over to the command post (CP) and went inside. A lieutenant, one of several guys sitting at radios along a long bench, got up, walked over, and shook my hand.

"Been expecting you, Lieutenant Bray," he said. "Top called and said you were on your way out. Going to Charlie Company, huh? Where you from?"

"Oklahoma," I replied.

"You'll like Charlie Company's CO (commanding officer); he's a good guy," the lieutenant said. "They got in some bad shit the other day. Just a minute, and I'll tell the battalion CO you're here." He disappeared down a long, sandbagged corridor.

The battalion's commanding officer, Lieutenant Colonel Price, whose name has been changed for the purposes of this memoir, strode back up the corridor. "Sergeant, where the hell is my goddamned C-and-C (command-and-control) ship?" he stormed as he walked into the command post. "That helicopter was supposed to be here an hour ago."

"I don't know, sir," replied the sergeant, who sat in front of the bank of radios. "They said it had to go to Bronco and refuel, sir, and then it would be right out."

Lieutenant Colonel Price turned to me. "What's your name, lieutenant?"

My freshly issued jungle fatigue shirt didn't have my name and rank on it. It would be a couple of days before Top sent one out. "Lieutenant Bray, sir," I replied.

"You're going to Charlie Company, right?" he asked.

"Yes, sir," I said.

"I'll tell you one goddamned thing, lieutenant," he said. "I don't want you to think that you can buddy-buddy with your men. There's too much of that shit going on around here. You understand?"

"Yes, sir," I replied.

Price looked back at the sergeant, and said, "Lieutenant, show Lieutenant—, uh, him, down to where Charlie Company's CP is."

The lieutenant and I walked out onto the LZ.

"Don't worry, he's a prick to everybody," the lieutenant said, grinning at me. "See that big bunker down there with the radio aerials sticking up? That's where you'll find Charlie Company's command post. I'd better get back in there and find a C-and-C ship, or there'll be hell to pay." He turned and walked back into the command post bunker.

My meeting with Charlie Company's CO was reassuring after my encounter with Lieutenant Colonel Price. The captain was a professional, compassionate soldier who made you feel at ease in his company.

"You meet the battalion commander?" he asked.

"Yes, sir," I replied.

He looked at me and grinned. "Don't worry, I'm the one who has to deal with him most of the time," he said. The captain told me about the patrol in the mountains and the death of the lieutenant I was replacing and the other men. "Every time you lose one of these guys or see them get torn up, you can't help but feel responsible," he said. "It's going to happen, and you can't stop it sometimes. Just do the best you can."

We talked for a while, and he sent for Sergeant Knowles.

"Sergeant Knowles is your platoon sergeant," the captain said. "He's been around quite a while, and you can depend on him a lot. If you need anything, just let me know."

I headed outside to meet Sergeant Knowles. After all the traveling from one place to the next and being shuffled from one unit to the other, I was about to assume the very personal responsibility of taking command of my own platoon.

Sergeant Knowles came walking up the trail from the bunker below the hill. I had expected an older man with E-6 sergeant stripes on his shoulders. Instead, what I saw was a nineteen-year-old kid recently promoted to E-5. What he saw was a twenty-year-old kid who had recently been promoted to second lieutenant. I quickly learned that the commanding officer's confidence in Sergeant Knowles wasn't misplaced. Six months of wading around in the swamps and jungle around LZ Liz had matured him far beyond his age. In the coming months, his experience and advice would help me a great deal. Like the company CO had told me, "Some of this stuff they can't teach you back in the States; you just have to learn it as you go." I had a lot to learn, and some of it would be painful.

The captain walked outside the bunker and introduced me to Sergeant Knowles. I picked up my pack and rifle, and we walked down the hill to the three bunkers that First Platoon occupied on the perimeter.

"I'd like to meet the platoon before dark, Sergeant Knowles," I said.

"Sure thing, sir. Some of the men are at the mess tent eating. How about 1800 hours here at bunker four?" he asked.

"That's fine," I said. "Come to think of it, I haven't eaten anything today myself."

We walked to the opposite side of Liz to the mess tent and ate a hot meal. That would be one of the best things about coming to Liz one week of each month: hot food.

I could think of much better circumstances under which a man would want to meet the platoon he was about to lead. I had no conception of what had happened to them on the patrol in the mountains, other than what I had been told by the captain. I hadn't participated in any battle with the enemy. I hadn't seen men killed in action or watched as explosives blew them apart.

The men were gathered behind the big bunker on the south side of Liz's perimeter. I was at once struck by how young they looked. In another time and place, they could have passed for a group of high school seniors. Most of them were nineteen years old. I did a quick head count and came up with eighteen men, not counting Sergeant Knowles and myself.

"Where are the rest of the men?" I asked Knowles.

"This is it, sir," he replied.

Being habitually understrength was an issue I would have to deal with for the next year. A normal rifle platoon consisted of thirty-four men: the headquarters unit, which included the platoon leader, platoon sergeant, and radio-telephone operator (RTO); two M-60 machine gun crews with a gunner and an assistant gunner in each; and three rifle squads made up of nine men each—the squad leader, two fire team leaders, two automatic riflemen, two riflemen, and two grenadiers. Even as early as the fall of 1969, there was talk of reducing American troop strength in Vietnam. Because of a lack of replacements, the platoon would never reach full strength. The most I would ever have would be twenty-six soldiers, and during one two-week period we would operate with only fourteen men, including myself.

I had often heard my father and uncle speak of the friendships and bonds they formed with the men they served with in the army. As I looked into the faces of these soldiers gathered around the bunker, I had no idea that thirty-five years later I would miss them as one would a brother. They represented young men from all across America. White, black, southerner, northerner, Spanish, American Indian, Italian, German, Irish. No matter our background, we would all share one common bond: we would spend the most defining time of our young lives in this place called Vietnam.

Directly in front of me was Steve "Stub" Fordice. Stub would make every step I made carrying a PRC-25 radio strapped to his pack. When the regular RTO rotated back to the States shortly after I took over the platoon, I asked for a volunteer to carry the radio. Stub stepped forward. A shy, quiet kid from Enterprise, Oregon, he was only five feet seven and weighed maybe one hundred and forty pounds. When I asked him if he was sure he wanted to carry the heavy radio and extra batteries, he replied, "No problem." He never complained. When I needed the radio, it was always a step away.

Leaning against the bunker was Boyd Lee Wade, a tall, dark-haired, quiet kid from Ringling, Oklahoma. He had spent his youth wandering up and down the Red River hunting and fishing. If ever there was a natural-born infantryman, he was one. He could walk forever carrying the heavy M-60 machine gun and five hundred rounds of belted ammunition. When the rest of the platoon would take a break on a long patrol and collapse to rest, Wade would stand leaning on his M-60 as if he were impatient to get started again. He was one of the few men I ever saw who could fire the heavy M-60 from the shoulder and be accurate with it. I never had to worry about his weapon jamming from being dirty. Each day he would disassemble, clean, and polish it.

Next was Ronald Embree. He could have been voted most popular in his high school class back in Iowa. Good humored, with a perpetual grin on his face, he was one of the most-liked men of the platoon. I never heard him say a cross word to any of the men. His squad was the most tightly knit. Of all the members of the platoon, he cared the most for the Vietnamese people. He would always carry extra C rations to hand out to the Vietnamese kids when we operated near them.

Sitting on a pile of sandbags was Steve "Doc" Miles, the platoon medic. The free-spirited young man from Washington, D.C., had grown up knowing that he wanted to join the military. When his medical training class had graduated at Fort Sam Houston, Texas, it received orders to go to Germany. Miles volunteered for duty in Vietnam. When he arrived, he weighed two hundred and ten pounds. He contracted dysentery and lost eighty-five pounds, though he never left the field. He was one of the most dedicated men I have ever known. On two occasions I saw him cry when he couldn't save the life of wounded people.

Next was Len Groom, a big, quiet kid from Ely, Minnesota. After high school he had gone to trade school to become a welder, which was what he was doing when he was drafted. It was hard to get him to say more than a few words at a time. Most often his response was simply "yes, sir" or "no, sir." He started as a rifleman but eventually wound up as an M-60 machine gunner.

Holding a letter from home was Sherman "Bo" Armstrong. Armstrong was always friendly and eager to help the new replacements feel at ease. We had grown up barely forty miles from each other back in Oklahoma. He liked to kid me about the fact that his high school had always beaten mine in football. One day I told him that wasn't much to brag about since everyone we played beat us. He must have felt bad about what he'd said, because he stopped mentioning it. A month or so later while we were on Liz, he and some of the other men tossed around a homemade football. As he ran through the grass to catch a pass, he tripped over a piss tube (an empty artillery shipping tube used to urinate in) that was stuck in the ground and went rolling through the grass. I happened to be walking by and caught him wiping the blood from a scrape on his shin.

"And to think that we let you beat us," I said and laughed as I continued up the trail. The kidding was back on.

Standing at the bunker entrance was Pvt. John O. Smith, a tall, skinny kid from Purdy, Missouri. He had spent his early life roaming the hills and backwoods hunting and fishing, not for sport, but to provide food for his family's table. During the time I knew him, I don't think he said a dozen words to me. He was slow to accept the friendship of the other men, but eventually he became good friends with Bo Armstrong and a few other members of his squad.

Finally, there was Tony Nunes, a small, skinny kid from Danbury, Connecticut. The thing I remember most about him was the look on his face as he sat there on the sandbags in the late afternoon sun. The horror of watching a bullet go through someone's head was still fresh in his mind.

My father, Avril Bray, was born and raised less than a mile from our farm in eastern Oklahoma. He served as part of the occupation forces in Japan—where this photo was taken in 1945—after America dropped atomic bombs on Hiroshima and Nagasaki to end World War II.

I'm standing in the doorway in this photo of my dad, sister, and two brothers.

My wife, Joyce, was on hand to celebrate my finishing basic training at Fort Polk, Louisiana, in the summer of 1968. We had been married less than a year. Ahead of me lay officer candidate school— and Vietnam.

Dennis Guthrie was my best friend in high school. He enlisted in the army a few months ahead of me. He was killed in action on January 23, 1969, while serving with the Ninth Infantry Division in Vietnam. *(Courtesy Clara Guthrie)*

Landing Zone (LZ) "Liz" sat almost directly in the middle of 515 Valley. This photograph documents my first impression of LZ Liz—a hill made of sandbags with the Stars and Stripes flying overhead. Liz was my home for the year I served in Vietnam.

This photo of LZ Liz, taken from the heliport, shows the bunkers that were the area's most noticeable feature. At the top of the hill in the background is the North OP (observation post).

I pause for a photograph during a break on patrol. Waist-high "elephant" grass covered the foothills, and transitioned abruptly into triple-canopy jungle.

Sgt. Eddie Knowles sits on the right, behind me. He was my platoon sergeant in First Platoon, Charlie Company. Though he was only nineteen, six months of wading around in the swamps and jungle had matured him far beyond his age. Knowles's experience and advice helped me a great deal.

"Tom" was Charlie Company's Vietnamese interpreter. In the background is the squad led by Ronald Embree, an Iowan, one of the most-liked men of the platoon. The dark-haired soldier to the right is Boyd Lee Wade, a quiet kid from Ringling, Oklahoma, who was a natural-born infantryman.

Resupply helicopters like this one were a welcome sight. Batteries, C rations, ammunition—whatever we needed—was delivered to wherever we camped. To the right, holding the radio handset, is Captain Donovan.

Like his predecessor, Captain Donovan was a professional, compassionate soldier who made you feel at ease in his company.

Members of First Platoon prepare to return to the field after stand-down at Chu Lai.

CHAPTER 7

The Gaza Strip

Sunday morning came, and Charlie Company's week on Liz would end the following day. A couple of days earlier, Captain Donovan had been assigned as our new company commander. Over the course of the next several months, I would come to like and respect him very much. Just before noon, Captain Donovan called me to the company command bunker, along with the other platoon leaders, and explained that at 0630 hours the next morning we would combat assault onto the Gaza Strip. Delta Company had been operating there during the previous week and had lost several men to snipers and booby traps. While the other lieutenants occasionally jotted a note, I tried to write down every word the captain spoke. To say I was a little apprehensive would have been the understatement of a lifetime.

Lieutenant Vinson, the Second Platoon leader, nudged me with his elbow and grinned. "You'll do fine."

Captain Donovan continued his briefing. Our mission would be to conduct daytime patrols and nightly ambushes to deny VC and NVA access to use the area as a supply base and staging area. Fire support would come from LZ Liz and LZ Bronco in the form of 155 mm and 105 mm artillery. Sharks from LZ Bronco and Warlords from the division headquarters at Chu Lai would supply helicopter gunship power. Also from Chu Lai, Helix OV-1 Birddogs (the call sign for an Air Force forward air controller flying in an OV-1), would provide fixed-wing aircraft air strikes.

Donovan continued, giving radio frequencies—or pushes—and call signs for all the supporting elements. Next he gave us a series of grid coordinates for the landing zone on the Gaza Strip, the company's expected day laager position (where the company rested and received helicopter resupply), cloverleaf patrol routes, and the company's expected NDP (night defensive position). Last, he told us predetermined and fixed-grid reference points, a series of fixed points on our maps that had been assigned various coded names to use over the radio instead of giving our exact position in the clear. The NVA had copies of the same maps we used, and more than once in the coming year a unit would be mortared immediately after giving its position in the clear, especially if it was operating near the mountains.

The captain finished his briefing by telling us to carry two days' rations and a full complement of ammunition. He was unsure whether we would receive supplies from a helicopter the next afternoon. My platoon would go in on the first lift, along with part of Second Platoon and the company command group.

I spent the afternoon checking and rechecking my notes from the captain and briefing the platoon on the coming operation. When I told the men we were going to the Strip, they seemed relieved.

"The Strip's bad enough, but at least they're not sending us back to those damn mountains," Private Nunes said.

"I've had enough of them, too," Knowles replied. "Hell, I'm too short for that kind of shit. Think you could get me a job in the rear this afternoon, sir?" Knowles grinned as he looked at the other men standing around him.

"I'll get right to work on that, Knowles," I said, "but I wouldn't hold my breath waiting for it."

"Guess I better get busy then, sir," he said as he walked off to check the men.

After I had done all that I knew to do, I walked up the hill to the command bunker and sat down outside the door. The sun was just beginning to set over the dark mountains at the mouth of 515 Valley. To the east, the pale blue waters of the South China Sea were visible over the Gaza Strip. That's where I would be when I saw the sun again. No more training, no more play-like aggressors, and no more chances to go back and try again if something went terribly wrong. Tomorrow it was all for keeps.

The eastern sky was beginning to turn a bright shade of pink. I had been up for two hours checking and rechecking the list I had made the previous afternoon: ammunition, canteens full of water, helmets, flak jackets, grenades, claymores (mines), light anti-tank weapons (LAWs), spare batteries for the PRC-25 radio, C rations, first-aid kits, insect repellent, C-4 explosives, blasting caps, fuse. The list seemed endless.

Charlie Company assembled in a small field near the access road entrance to Liz waiting for the Dolphins (the call sign for Huey helicopters) to arrive from LZ Bronco. As I looked over the company in the early morning light, the armament was impressive. Nine M-60 machine guns with thousands of rounds of belt-linked ammunition; LAWs that fired a 66 mm rocket from a disposable tube; more than a hundred men carrying M-16 rifles, each with two hundred rounds of ammunition. The company could fire more than twenty-five thousand rounds of small-arms ammunition in a matter of minutes. It was hard to imagine that the Viet Cong would even challenge such a heavily armed and formidable force.

I walked over to Sergeant Knowles. He and a few other members of First Platoon were sitting in the grass, leaning back on their rucksacks, laughing at a joke one of the men had told. They seemed relaxed and loose.

"Everything ready, Knowles?" I asked.

"Yes, sir," he replied as he stood up and looked over the platoon spread out in the field. "I've got the men broken down into six-man groups like we planned last night."

"Okay," I replied. "Captain Donovan just called and said the choppers were lifting off from Bronco. They'll be here in a few minutes. Tell the men to get lined up."

"Yes, sir," he said. "Remember, lieutenant—keep your head down."

"You don't have to tell me twice," I said, then walked over to Stub's position where the lead chopper would touch down.

In the distance to the southeast, we could hear the big guns on Bronco firing salvo after salvo. From the east came the deep rumbling sound of the 105 mm and 155 mm shells as they exploded on the landing zone in the Strip where we would land in a few minutes.

The six Hueys came into view over the east side of the South OP. They flew in a formation of two parallel lines of three each, resembling a flying rectangle. Off to the side of the slicks (Hueys), two Shark helicopter gunships circled, waiting for the slicks to pick us up. Someone from the company command post tossed a smoke grenade between the first two groups of men waiting for the choppers. It popped and hissed, then bright yellow clouds of smoke poured out as it lay in the grass. The slicks swung around and started their approach to us from the east, aiming at the location indicated by the grenade. Their rotor blades made a deafening roar as they neared the ground. Grass and debris swirled and filled the air from the downwash as they came to a hover, then settled to the ground. We climbed aboard. Some of the men sat on the metal floor, while others climbed into the nylon webbing seats, facing the front and rear of the helicopter. I sat on the floor along the side by the open door, with my feet resting on the outside landing struts.

We lifted off, leaving the rest of the company to await the slicks' return. We gained altitude and headed north up Highway 1, then made a slow turn eastward toward the South China Sea. The air rushing through the open doors of the helicopter was cool. For some reason, I looked over behind the door gunner and noticed that he was strapped to the helicopter by a short, wide nylon belt. He noticed me looking and gave me a big grin. I didn't see much humor in the reason for the nylon belt. As we approached the LZ, the door gunner three feet to my left suddenly opened up with the swivel-mounted M-60 machine gun. I nearly jumped out of the helicopter. I watched the path of the tracers as they found their way into the brush and stands of bamboo and realized that he was only putting down suppressive fire.

The dark gray smoke from the artillery fire drifted inland away from the LZ. The soldiers manning the artillery had stopped firing as we made our turn toward the sea. The shell craters were visible, some with little white wisps of smoke rising from the center. The ground below looked to be old abandoned rice paddies. Short brush had grown up along the dikes, with occasional thick stands of bamboo twenty feet tall. To the east, a dense tree line of saltwater cedars obscured any view of the ground.

The slicks touched down. I jumped from the strut before it hit the ground and raced to a paddy dike a few meters away. Stub followed with the radio. The helicopters again raised a cloud of dust and debris as they lifted off for the return flight to Liz to pick up the remainder of the company. It grew eerily quiet as the slicks disappeared back to the west. The only sound was the rotor noise of the two Sharks overhead patrolling a large circle around our perimeter. Thankfully, there was no gunfire. I searched the brush and bamboo for any signs of movement. The men had formed a rough defensive perimeter approximately one hundred meters in diameter. Sergeant Knowles was directly across from me on the other side. Our orders were to remain in position until the rest of the company arrived. I had no problem with that. From all the possible Viet Cong hiding places I could see, I was in no hurry to move from the protection of my paddy dike.

I saw Captain Donovan to the east of my position a few meters away. I low-crawled over to where he was talking on the radio. He told the rest of the company and the battalion command post that we had received negative contact and were waiting for the rest of the company. After he finished on the radio, he looked over at me and said, "Well, Lieutenant Bray, what do you think about your first combat assault?"

"Not too bad, sir, as long as we don't start getting shot at," I replied.

"As soon as the rest of the company gets here, I'll brief you on the patrols for the day," he said. "Just stay loose for a while."

"Yes, sir." I crawled back over to where Stub and Sergeant Eddy lay looking out into the brush.

The Dolphins made two more lifts and brought the rest of the company to the strip. They landed west of Captain Donovan's position and consolidated the rest of the perimeter. People were up and walking around, so I felt much better about the situation than I had an hour earlier.

The commanding officer sent word for me and the other platoon leaders to join him at the command post. He briefed us on the operation for the remainder of the day, an assignment I would hear virtually every day for the coming year: patrol. Because my platoon was on the left flank, I would patrol due south for three "clicks" (one thousand meters equals one click) and then west for one click to join up with the rest of the company at the NDP. The country was relatively open, so I put the men in three columns abreast, separated by about fifty meters. I would walk near the front of the middle column and Sergeant Knowles would be near the rear. Before we moved out, Knowles admonished the men to keep a twenty-meter interval. We started moving south. By now the sun was up and getting hotter. Most of the men removed their fatigue jackets and donned army-issue green T-shirts. Before we had moved far, the T-shirts turned a dark shade of green from perspiration.

We moved slowly, the point man in each column scanning the ground in front for the telltale sign of a trip wire or pressure-type firing device indicating a mine or booby trap. The second and third men scanned the area ahead and to the sides for any enemy movement. The countryside was beautiful and frightening at the same time. I was unaccustomed to the banana trees, the tall slender stalks of bamboo, and the lush vegetation that seemed to grow in every direction. At the same time, the beauty of the countryside provided an endless supply of hiding places for the people who wanted nothing more than to kill or maim us.

We had moved more than a click south when I got my first look at a little Vietnamese village. The village was located on a small, elevated piece of ground surrounded by banana trees and bamboo. I was struck by the simplicity of everything. For someone accustomed to housing structures in the United States, residences in the village were primitive, indeed. Thatch walls and roofs, lean-tos built of sticks and branches, and hard-packed dirt floors were a novelty to me. When I looked inside one of the huts, I was equally surprised to see how crudely the people there lived. A few pots hanging on the wall, a platform made of bamboo covered by a rice straw mat for sleeping, and an open fire in one corner for cooking. An American home would have been stuffed full of furniture, rugs, appliances, food, clothing, and all the other things deemed necessities. In Vietnam, things seemed to be stripped to survival mode.

About halfway through the village, I saw my first Vietnamese peasants. Sergeant Eddy's squad had uncovered the entrance to a bunker when the soldiers heard a child crying inside. Two or three of the men pointed their weapons into the bunker, hollering, "*Lai dai, lai dai,*" the Vietnamese words for "come here." About a dozen old men, women, and children filed out of the bunker. We had no way to communicate with them, as the company interpreter was with the commanding officer.

Doc Miles said to them, "VC, VC," and pointed into the surrounding countryside.

"No VC, no VC," they said. Throughout the year I was in Vietnam, the peasants never knew anything about the VC. I suppose I couldn't blame them. If they told us anything, they would have likely been executed that night, along with the rest of their families.

One of the old Vietnamese women walked over to the entrance of another bunker and spoke in Vietnamese. Another eight or ten old people emerged. Their reply was the same, "No VC, no VC." I noticed one old woman bleeding from the mouth. I was about to call Doc Miles over to treat her, figuring she had been hit by some of the shrapnel from the morning's bombardment, when Private Nunes informed me that she was chewing betel nut. It was the Vietnamese equivalent of chewing tobacco, only the juice was as bright red as blood. The old Vietnamese women were fond of the stuff.

I told Sergeant Knowles to take Embree's squad and search the village. I was surprised when he grabbed one of the old women and started dragging her off toward one of the hooches.

"What are you doing, Knowles?" I asked.

"Sir, if you take one of them with you and there are booby traps, they usually freak out when you get close to it."

"That makes sense," I said, feeling a little stupid. Lesson one for a green lieutenant.

The search of the village turned up nothing. By the time we left to continue the patrol, the little children had gotten over their fear of us and were begging for candy and food. I looked back to see Embree passing out the contents of a C ration box as we moved out of the village. The sweet, half-sickening smell of the village remained in my nostrils—a combination of sweat, cooked rice, incense, and smoke. All the villages smelled the same. Smelling that scent in the mountains meant the NVA was close.

We neared the south end of our patrol and got ready to turn west and link up with the company. I turned and told Stub to give me the handset on the radio so I could call the CO and tell him our position. As I reached for the handset, I heard crack-thump, crack-thump. The whole platoon hit the ground as if their feet had struck a giant trip wire.

"Are you okay, sir?" Stub asked.

"I think so," I replied. "Was that what I think it was, Stub?"

"Yes, sir," he replied, as we crawled to the protection of a little clump of bamboo growing on a small hill.

"It came from that tree line to the east, didn't it, Stub?" I asked.

"I think so, sir."

Behind and to my left, Wade's M-60 fired a long burst in that direction. I looked through the six-power scope on my M-14 at a solid wall of vegetation. Directly in front of my position, an overgrown ravine led toward the tree line from which the sniper was firing. I looked to my left and saw Sergeant Knowles running in a crouched position to where Embree's squad was located. He dove behind the paddy dike where Private Adkins lay with his M-79 grenade launcher. I yelled for Sergeant Eddy to bring his squad up to the ravine on my right. Adkins's M-79 blooped three times. Small gray clouds erupted in the trees where the grenades landed. A few of the men of Embree's squad fired short bursts from their M-16s. I told Stub to wait behind the bamboo thicket for Eddy's squad to come up. I bent as low to the ground as I could and ran the fastest forty-yard dash of my life to where Sergeant Knowles lay behind the dike.

"You see anything, Knowles?" I asked and retrieved my helmet, which had come off as I dove beside him.

"No, sir, they're probably hidden in spider holes under the tree line. At this distance, you won't ever be able to spot them."

Just then, a geyser of dirt erupted in the field in front of us as another bullet ricocheted over our heads. I ducked my head below the dike while Knowles continued to watch the tree line. "Get your head down before you get it shot off, Knowles," I said.

"I'm trying to spot the little bastard. Besides, they can't hit shit at this distance," he said, still watching.

Adkins fired another round from the M-79. The 40 mm grenade made a loud "crump" sound as it landed in the branches of a tree in the distant tree line. I was not so confident of their bad marksmanship after hearing what had happened a week and a half before in the mountains.

"I'll take Eddy's squad down the ravine and try to work closer to them while you keep Embree's and Adam's squads here to cover us," I told Knowles.

He looked over to the right at the ravine leading toward the tree line. "I wouldn't do that, sir. That's exactly what they want you to do. You go down that ditch, some people are going to get blown up. That's probably why they waited till we got here to shoot at us. You can bet your ass that there are four or five booby traps or maybe a command-detonated claymore in there."

The logic of what he said hit home immediately. Lesson number two for the day. If I couldn't go to where the VC was, I knew something that could. I jumped to my feet and ran hard back to Stub's position. The men stopped firing, and it grew eerily quiet. The only sound was the buzzing of an insect in the bamboo thicket.

Sergeant Eddy looked at me and said, "The men are ready, sir. What do you want me to do?" I motioned for Stub to hand me the radio handset. "Change of plan, Sergeant Eddy. Just hang loose." I pushed the talk button on the handset and said, "Foxtrot niner-one, this is Charlie four-four, fire mission, over."

A voice from LZ Bronco, eight kilometers to the south, came back over the handset. "Charlie four-four, this is Foxtrot niner-one, ready, over."

"Foxtrot niner-one, this is Charlie four-four, target grid 81404565, range five hundred meters, direction eight-zero degrees, Victor Charlie in tree line, request one round whiskey papa, will adjust, over," I spoke into the handset.

The voice on the other end answered, "Charlie four-four, wait," followed in a few seconds by "Shot-out." The 105 mm shell exploded with a huge bang, shattering the quiet twenty-five meters short of the tree line. A mushrooming white cloud of smoke, surrounded by white streamers falling back to earth, marked the impact.

I squeezed the handset again. "Foxtrot niner-one, this is Charlie four-four, add five-zero meters and fire for effect, over."

The voice on the other end spoke my call sign and added, "Roger, over."

In a few seconds, the tree line erupted in a great cloud of smoke and dirt as the 105 mm explosive rounds impacted into it. Some of the rounds sent limbs and debris from the treetops flying to the ground.

Stub grinned, saying, "That'll teach the little bastards to shoot at us."

I had the Fire Direction Center (FDC) at Bronco walk the shells two hundred meters north down the tree line. When they were finished, I called them and thanked them for the mission.

"Glad to help," came the reply. "Let us know if we got any of 'em."

I got the platoon back in formation, and we cautiously approached the tree line. We found nothing but a couple of tracks, headed north, in the sandy dirt.

"You can bet your ass they were running when that Willie Peter (white phosphorous) hit in front of them," Knowles said.

"Looks like they headed north back to that village we passed earlier," I said.

"It's probably where they live, but remember, sir, those people don't know a damn thing about any VC shit."

We skirted the ravine and headed west the fifteen hundred meters to the company day laager position. When we arrived, I told the men to relax, and I walked over to the shade of a stand of banana trees where Captain Donovan's CP was located.

He looked up from the log he was sitting on. "Run into a little stuff over there, Lieutenant Bray?"

"Yes, sir," I replied. "I don't much care for the sound of a bullet going by me."

"It'll scare the hell out of you as bad in six months as it does now," he said. "You don't ever get used to that sound."

I gave him a report on the patrol—searching the village, the snipers, and the fire mission.

"I know," he said. "I was monitoring all of it on the radio. You handled the situation well with the snipers. Better to let the artillery or gunships flush 'em out rather than risk your men."

I admitted to him that I had gotten some good advice from Sergeant Knowles.

"He's a good man," Donovan said. "He's got more experience out here than you and I have. Just keep listening and learning. Your platoon need anything on resupply? We're going to get a resupply bird in before we move to the NDP."

"I don't think so, sir, but I'll check and let you know in a few minutes."

I walked back to First Platoon's position. It didn't take the men long to relax. They had shed their rucksacks, flak jackets, and boots and were sitting or lying in the shade of the trees. Some napped, while others talked or listened to music on their transistor radios. The day's patrol was history to them. They were busy talking about girls, cars, and how short some of them were. I found it humorous when John Smith remarked that he only had 355 days left. He and I had a ways to go. We had arrived at First Platoon on the same day.

The resupply chopper arrived at 1730 hours. The only thing my platoon had ordered was a few cases of C rations and ammunition to replace what we had fired at the snipers. Willy Lewis ordered batteries for his flashlight. I knew they were for his tape player. I didn't think he even carried a flashlight, but if we could spend ten thousand dollars' worth of artillery ammunition on one VC sniper, a couple of dollars' worth of batteries for the kid to listen to his music seemed reasonable to me.

As soon as the resupply ship lifted off, the company began to move to the NDP. The captain had selected a spot to the northeast around an old abandoned pagoda. After establishing a perimeter, the men began to dig defensive positions and foxholes. Two squads from each platoon would be sent out on "snakes," or ambushes, at varying distances from the NDP. I sent Embree's squad to the northeast to an old, abandoned, blown up bridge across the Cau River. Sergeant Eddy's squad would go directly north near another old pagoda situated beside a well-used trail that ran down the length of the strip. The remaining squad would stay with me at the company location to act as a reaction force in case one of the snakes ran into trouble. There was a dusk-to-dawn curfew in force throughout the battalion's area of operation. Anyone who moved after dark was considered to be the enemy.

I spent my first night in the field staring through the lens of a starlight scope (a battery-operated night vision device that amplified the available light from the stars and moon) and listening for any sound that might indicate the Viet Cong were approaching our perimeter. It was hard to hear sounds in the distance because of the constant buzz from the hordes of mosquitoes flying around my head. I hadn't known there were that many mosquitoes in the world! Stub had warned me to use a liberal amount of "bug juice" before dark. Now I could see why. They hadn't been nearly as bad on Liz. Just to the east of the perimeter, the river backed up into a low-lying area to form a stagnant water swamp, which provided good protection from the VC. In retrospect, I would have preferred them to the clouds of mosquitoes.

Stub and I took turns on watch and monitoring the radio. Embree and Eddy called in every hour on the radio with a "sit-rep" (situation report), to let us know that they were okay. I finally gave up any thought of trying to sleep while Stub was on watch. I hoped the next 354 nights wouldn't be like this one.

Pink sky appeared over the hill to the east. Dawn disclosed that what I had thought several times during the night was a Viet Cong was actually the headstone on a grave by the old pagoda. The first rays of sunlight sent the mosquitoes in search of their daytime hiding places in the swamp and bamboo thickets. One moment they were everywhere and the next you couldn't see one. My arms, face, and neck felt like I had rubbed them with axle grease. I would never get used to the smell and oily feeling of the army-issued insect repellant.

Embree and Eddy returned with their squads from the night's ambushes. The company had sent out eight snakes with negative contact. The VC knew we were in the area.

After the other snakes had closed on the NDP, the company moved southeast two clicks to higher ground in the saltwater cedar thickets.

Captain Donovan called the platoon leaders to the CP.

"Give the men three or four hours to sleep and eat," he stated. "This afternoon we will cloverleaf the area with patrols. Colonel Price has been flying around the area and thinks that the Viet Cong who hit Delta Company last week may be using a village on the coast down south of here. Nothing definite yet, but we may be doing a cordon and search at dawn in a day or two. Come back at 1300 hours, and I'll give you your patrol routes."

As I turned to head back to First Platoon's position, Lieutenant Vinson said, "Hey Bray, were the mosquitoes bad at your position last night?"

I raised my T-shirt and showed him the welts on my back.

"Me, too," he said.

Back with the platoon, I told Knowles the plan for the day.

"Good," he said. "I need some sleep after last night."

"Me, too," I said. When I told him about the possible cordon and search, he reacted angrily.

"That's a bunch of bullshit, sir. Moving around here in the dark is number ten."

"Number ten" meant bad. I didn't question his judgment. He hadn't been wrong yet. I found shade next to a banana tree and made a pallet with my poncho liner. The last twenty-nine hours were beginning to catch up with me. A cool breeze blew in off the South China Sea. Through a small gap in the trees, you could barely see the waves breaking on the distant shore. I went to sleep quickly.

What seemed like seconds later, Stub nudged my arm. "Sir, it's 1230 hours. You said to wake you up."

"Thanks, Stub," I said, trying to focus in the brilliant light. My shade had moved while I slept, and the day was oppressively hot. I made my way back to the company CP. The captain assigned me to a patrol route southwest to the river, east one click, and then back northwest to the day laager. He said we would probably remain in our present position for the night.

I got the platoon together and moved out toward the river. We used the same formation as the day before, as the terrain remained relatively open. The trip to the river was uneventful. When we reached its banks, I told the men to take a break. There wasn't much danger of being shot at there since there wasn't any cover within rifle range.

Private Wade sat down beside me on the riverbank. "Are we going to be here a few minutes, sir?"

"Yeah, maybe fifteen minutes," I said.

He pulled off his boots and waded out a few feet into the ankle-deep clear water flowing over the sand. "This is kinda like the Red River back in Oklahoma, sir. I used to take my fishing pole and walk down the river from one deep hole to the next, fishing all day."

"Yeah, Wade," I replied. "The only thing is back in Oklahoma we didn't have to worry about some little bastard shooting at us from the bank."

He grinned and put his boots back on. I liked the tall, dark-headed kid. As I would find out in the coming months, we shared a lot of similarities in our growing-up years.

We moved eastward from the river. We had barely started when we heard a muffled explosion to the northeast. In a few seconds, an excited voice came over the radio requesting an urgent Dust Off. Third Platoon had hit a booby trap on its patrol. It reported three "Whiskey India Alpha" (wounded in action). One of the men had suffered traumatic amputation of both legs at the knees. The other two had received shrapnel wounds to the abdomen and chest. From the sound of it, the point man had tripped the mine. In a few moments, a Huey with red crosses painted on its sides flew over our heads en route toward the beach. After a few more minutes, we watched as it made its return flight to Bronco carrying the three wounded soldiers. The mood of the men became somber.

As we patrolled eastward, we came to a stand of trees surrounding a small, deserted Vietnamese village. Only a couple of hooches remained, and one of those was half burned. Nearby, piles of ashes indicated where other hooches had once stood. A pair of game chickens scratched in the ashes, causing small clouds of black dust to rise over their backs. The fires had been relatively recent, likely the result of Delta Company's visit to the area the week before. Expended shell casings lay near an old well in the center of the ruins. I picked one of them up and showed it to Stub.

"AK," he said, taking the piece of brass and rolling it between his fingers.

"Lieutenant, we got something over here," Embree yelled from near a stand of small trees. I walked over to his position, and he pointed to an eighteen-inch-diameter hole near the base of one of the trees.

"Wade spotted it, sir. He was walking by and felt that give under his foot," Embree said. He pointed to a round, woven mat of bamboo laced with dried bamboo leaves that had been used to cover the entrance to the tunnel.

Wade stood nearby. "I'm glad it wasn't booby-trapped," he said. "I felt it slide when I stepped on the side of it."

I eased up to the hole and looked down inside, keeping my M-14 pointed at the entrance. There was water in the bottom, with sharp stakes pointing upward. About four feet down, another tunnel headed north, perpendicular to the entrance.

Sergeant Knowles joined us there.

"Any tunnel rats in the platoon, sergeant?" I asked. I had heard vivid tales from the Rangers back at Fort Benning about men taking a .45 caliber pistol and a flashlight into the tunnels to search for VC and weapons caches. Maybe I wasn't as macho as the Rangers. I wasn't about to go in that tunnel. The water and the punji stakes were enough for me, plus the fact that I hated snakes. The inside of that tunnel looked like the perfect place for one to be hiding.

"No, sir," Knowles answered. "We usually throw in a couple of hand grenades and some CS (tear gas). If that doesn't work, we blow them with C-4."

"Okay, Knowles, that's what we'll do," I said. If I weren't going to go down there, I sure wouldn't ask one of my men to do it. I called the CO and told him we had found a tunnel. He instructed us to blow it in place. We moved back, and one of the men walked up near the tunnel, pulled the pin on a grenade, tossed it inside the hole, and ran for cover. I had the other men watch the surrounding area for signs of other entrances from the explosion. The grenade exploded with a loud boom and a shower of water. I walked up to the hole and looked inside. The only thing the grenade had accomplished was to blow out the water and destroy the punji stakes.

I pulled a grenade off my pistol belt, pulled the pin, and tossed it as far as I could down the horizontal tunnel leading off the entrance hole, then ran back to where Stub and Knowles stood crouched behind one of the old hooches. The grenade exploded, sending a cloud of dirt up the hole. I approached the hole again and looked inside. The roof of the tunnel hadn't even caved in where the grenade exploded. Knowles came over.

"We're going to need something a lot bigger than grenades to blow that thing up, Knowles," I said. "All I have is two pounds of C-4 with me, but I know something that will work."

While I had been on Liz one afternoon, I had noticed some forty-pound shaped charges stacked in the ammo bunker. Forty pounds of solid TNT molded into the shape of inverted ice cream cones. When they exploded, their shape caused them to concentrate the entire blast wave into a small area, the same as the armor-piercing rounds fired by tanks. They were capable of burning a hole through twelve inches of solid steel.

I called LZ Liz and requested two of the charges and some time fuse and blasting caps. Twenty minutes later, a Huey landed and dropped off the explosives. We carried them to the mouth of the tunnel. I jumped down into the hole, and Embree handed me the charges.

"You might as well crawl back in there, sir, and take a look around."

"No thanks, Embree, but if you want to, I'll loan you my pistol and flashlight," I said.

"Maybe Nunes will go in; he's the smallest guy in the platoon," Embree said, glancing at Private Nunes standing nearby.

"Screw that," Nunes said. He moved a few paces away.

I placed one of the charges on its side, facing down the horizontal tunnel. I put the other on its legs, facing the bottom of the entrance hole. The built-in legs on the charges were designed to hold the charge away from the target the proper distance so the blast wave could form. I rigged the shaped charges with blasting caps and connected them with detonating cord so they would explode simultaneously. I cut a five-foot length of fuse cord and placed a blasting cap on the end and inserted it, facing downward, into the back end of the charge. An odor similar to that in the village was seeping out of the horizontal tunnel, mixed with the smell of TNT from the grenades. I had Sergeant Knowles move all the men south two hundred meters to a low sand dune before Embree and I lit the fuse. We joined the rest of the platoon and waited. The fuse burned one foot per minute. I stared at my watch, waiting as the time for the explosion neared. BOOM-KABOOM! The ground erupted in a huge geyser of reddish-brown dirt, surrounding a mushrooming cloud of brilliant white smoke.

"Did you hear two explosions?" I asked Knowles, who stood beside me watching the smoke rise into the afternoon sky.

"I sure as hell did," he said. "Eighty pounds of TNT wouldn't make that big an explosion."

We moved back to where the tunnel had been. A crater fifteen feet in diameter and eight to ten feet deep marked where the tunnel entrance had been. The old hooch that had stood nearby was gone, as were the trees that had been close to the entrance. The ground to the north of the crater had caved in for one hundred feet, indicating the direction the tunnel had run.

"That sure as hell beats crawling down in there," Knowles said.

"I think so too, Knowles," I said. "If there was anybody down there, it'll take him a few days to dig his way out—if he's still alive."

The shaped charges would become my method for dealing with tunnels. Over the coming months, we would witness some spectacular secondary explosions. As we reformed to continue our patrol, I hoped the picture I had taken with my 35 mm camera turned out. I had snapped the shot just as the dirt erupted.

We returned to the company day laager position without incident. When we arrived, I went over to Captain Donovan to ask about the men from Third Platoon who had hit the booby trap. He told me that they were bad off, but he thought that they would live. The kid with his legs blown off hadn't been in country long.   ·

While I was at the CP, the captain told me there would be no patrols or snakes the following day. The battalion commander had decided that before dawn on Thursday the company would cordon and search the village on the beach. We had the rest of the day and the next to catch up on sleep. Only one snake from each platoon would go out that night. The following day, he would brief the platoon leaders on Thursday's operation. When I told Sergeant Knowles about Thursday's plan, his only reply was "damn."

The captain unfolded his map under the shade of his poncho liner, which had been stretched between four bamboo poles stuck into the sandy ground. He pointed to two villages twenty-five hundred meters south of our position called Ban An 1 and Ban An 2. The Vietnamese had abandoned the villages and combined them into one village to the east on the shore of the South China Sea. He had flown over the area the previous day with the battalion commander and said that from the air it appeared there were perhaps two hundred people living there. Military intelligence and information from a "Chieu Hoi" (a VC who had voluntarily changed sides) indicated that at least a platoon of Viet Cong was using the village as a base and sanctuary.

The plan was to move out at 0200 hours in the morning and establish a three-sided box around the village by 0430 hours. The sea would form the fourth side of the box, as the village was close to the shore. In effect, we would be laying a company-size ambush to kill any of the VC who might have spent the night in the village. In order to minimize the possibility of friendly units bumping into each other in the dark, the company would move south in a single column. My platoon would lead and be responsible for turning left past the village to seal off the south side of the box. Third Platoon would follow mine and seal off the west side of the box, while Second Platoon would do the same on the north. After daylight we would move into the village to search it. If all went according to plan, our predawn ambushes would kill several of the VC. We would move south through the cedar thickets to avoid detection.

We were ready to move out by 0130 hours. A half-moon was already beginning its descent into the western sky. Dark clouds floated across it, reducing visibility to a few feet. Six kilometers to the south we could see the generator-driven lights of LZ Bronco. They would give us a reference point as we tried to find our way south. To the east you could barely hear the surf breaking on the beach. I put Sergeant Eddy's squad on the point. I would walk the fourth man back, followed by Stub, to have better control of our direction. Private Armstrong would lead, carrying a Winchester pump shotgun loaded with buckshot. Behind Stub, Patrick O'Doud and Smith formed an M-60 machine gun crew.

Stub handed me the handset of the PRC-25. It was Captain Donovan, instructing us to move out. We would parallel the beach in the salt brush thickets. In places we would have to physically push our way through. While many well-worn trails existed, taking one of those routes invited the same fate that had happened to the three men of Third Platoon. Walking down the tree line on the beach would be even more dangerous. We had moved only a couple hundred yards when in the distance the sound of two gunshots rang out several hundred meters to our south.

"There goes the big surprise," Stub said in a low voice.

"What do you mean, Stub?" I asked.

"That's the VC's signal for warning the area that the Americans are coming."

We heard no further sounds from the south. We continued to work our way through the thick brush. Occasionally we would come to areas where it thinned out, and then we made better time. Other times it would become so thick that we would have to back up and go around. I could imagine the accordion effect this must have been having on the column of more than one hundred men stretched out behind me.

We were getting close to the village. I looked at the luminous dials of my watch: 0345 hours. We had passed the bombed-out shell of a pagoda six hundred meters back up the beach. Another was barely visible just to my left. They were the landmarks that were to let me know when we were even with the village. Another three hundred meters, and I would turn First Platoon to the left toward the beach. We were preparing to cross a wide trail that came from the area of the village when I saw Armstrong wheel to his left and drop to one knee, bringing the shotgun to his shoulder. The other men stopped and dropped to prone firing positions. I heard the metallic click of a safety being released, then a voice speaking Vietnamese. I crawled forward to Armstrong's position. He gestured with his hand for someone to come over to him. A few meters down the dark trail stood an old Vietnamese man dressed in white, holding the hand of a young child. He murmured in Vietnamese as he slowly approached.

"I saw something moving out of the corner of my eye, sir, and they just walked right up on me before they saw me. They didn't try to run and didn't have a weapon, so I didn't know what to do," Armstrong explained in a low voice.

I walked over to the old man. He was shaking and crying. The child wrapped his arms around the old man's leg. The old man put his hand in his pocket. I pointed my M-14 at his chest and flipped off the safety with my forefinger. He pulled out a plastic ID card issued by the South Vietnamese government. I took the card and looked at the picture on the front. He clasped his hands under his chin, muttering in Vietnamese, bowing his head again and again. I gave him back the card and pointed down the trail away from the village.

"*Di di mau,*" I said to him.

He took the kid by the hand and disappeared down the trail.

One of the men lying nearby said, "You should have blown the old bastard away, Armstrong."

"I ain't shootin' no kid," he said.

I told Armstrong to move out back to the south.

We hadn't moved fifty meters when the roar of automatic weapons fire shattered the quiet of predawn. Everything moved in slow motion. Ahead and on each side of Armstrong, I could see the muzzle flashes of two weapons, as though someone had pointed a blowtorch at me. I dove to the ground, but gravity stopped. I seemed to float to the ground. I could hear the bullets ripping into the trees around me. One kicked a shower of sand beside me. I pointed my rifle forward, but I couldn't see Armstrong and the other man with him. I heard his shotgun roar. One, two, three, four, five times, then silence. I lay there a few seconds.

"Armstrong, are you okay?" I asked into the darkness.

"I think so if I can get my heart to start beating again," he answered.

I breathed a sigh of relief. "You see anything?"

"No, sir, I think they hauled ass."

We slowly got to our feet. I did a quick headcount and checked on the men. Miraculously, no one had been hit. Ahead we found two piles of spent brass. A few feet behind the brass, Smith found a tree limb with blood on it. Maybe Armstrong's shotgun had found its target.

We moved to our assigned positions on the south side of the village and waited for dawn. From the high sand dunes, I could make out the silhouette of the hooches on the beach.

Sergeant Knowles came over to where I was lying in the sand beside a machine gun position. "I told you it wasn't a good idea to go marching around out here in the dark," he said.

I agreed with him. I didn't care if we ever tried anything like that again.

The sun came up a brilliant red ball over the ocean. We hadn't seen any VC leave the village. They had left well before we got there. Near the village, we could see smoke rising from early morning cooking fires. I was still trying to figure out why the old man had been on the path with the kid. Embree walked over to us. We were talking about moving into the village when he reached over and lifted the shoulder strap of my rucksack.

"What's this?" he asked.

I looked and saw a perfectly round hole through the strap near where it was connected to the pack.

"Damn, sir, that was close," he said quietly.

I rubbed the strap between my fingers, feeling the round hole the bullet had made a couple of hours earlier. Only four days in country and twice bullets had come close to sending me home. The little round hole in the green strap would become just another of my images of Vietnam.

We moved into the village and searched it. All the villagers were gathered up and questioned by "Tom," our company Vietnamese interpreter. As expected, not one of them knew anything about the Viet Cong. We had been ambushed three hundred meters away, but they knew nothing.

"They lie. Many VC here," Tom told Captain Donovan. A few of the middle-aged men and young boys were put on helicopters and sent to military intelligence for questioning. After a couple of hours, the company pulled out and moved a kilometer down the beach.

We spent the next two weeks patrolling and conducting night ambushes on the strip. When we came back for another rotation, we wouldn't have to worry about cordoning and searching the village anymore. It wouldn't be there. The battalion had lost so many men out there that brigade headquarters and the South Vietnamese provincial governor decided to make a free-fire zone out of the Gaza Strip. All the Vietnamese inhabitants would be gathered up and moved to pacified villages along Highway 1. Eventually, bulldozers would be brought in and the strip would be cleared of all vegetation. Once an area is declared a free-fire zone, anyone spotted within its boundaries is considered to be hostile and may be fired upon without following the usual rules of engagement. Even with that, many more American boys would lose their lives or be maimed there.

I had survived my first three-week rotation in the field, and none of my men had been hurt. On our last day in the field before we began our week of pulling security for Liz, we received word our company would get a three-day stand down at the American Division headquarters in Chu Lai. That meant three days of no guard duty, and a chance to shop at the division post exchange (PX) and relax.

We were ordered to march from the strip to Bronco for the flight to Chu Lai. Halfway to Bronco, after we crossed the river, I saw great black and gray clouds headed toward the coast from over the mountains to the west. I had been there four weeks, and it hadn't rained. We had just crossed the one-hundred-meter-wide Tra Cau River and barely gotten our ankles wet. It began to rain—not just a steady rain, but sheets of rain mixed with a chilling wind off the mountains. I had grown accustomed to one hundred–plus degree temperatures, and when it dropped into the sixties, I shivered as the wind blew the cold rain under my poncho and down my neck. At times I could only see fifty meters ahead.

We took a break in a stand of trees. I opened a pound cake I had saved from a C ration, and by the time I got the lid off with my little can opener, the contents had turned to mush. I drank the pound cake. Stub leaned against a tree, his head under his poncho, trying to light a cigarette.

"How long do these thunderstorms last?" I asked him.

"This ain't no thunderstorm, sir. You'll be wadin' in mud up to your ass for the next five or six months. This is October, the start of the monsoon season."

He was right. It would rain nearly every day and night for the next five months. We finished our march to Bronco like he said, wading and splashing through the mud.

Four giant, double-blade Chinook helicopters picked up the company at Bronco and carried us to Chu Lai that afternoon. We checked in our weapons at an armory and were assigned barracks near the center of the huge base. At the mess hall, the company provided free beer, iced down in barrels, and a steak dinner, our first hot meal in three weeks. The next day the men went to the base PX and lazed around drinking beer. I headed over to the airstrip and watched the F-4 fighter jets being loaded with bombs and napalm.

They were constantly taking off and landing, coming and going from air strikes around northern Vietnam. Nearby was the parking area for the "Blue Ghost" Cobra gunships. It was my first opportunity to get close to one of the menacing helicopters. One of the pilots saw me admiring it and came out to talk. He explained the operation of the mini-gun in the nose and the rocket launchers under the stubby wings. I was glad the VC and NVA didn't have anything like it.

That night the company was treated with a show from an Australian rock band. That night also marked the first and last time I ever drank in Vietnam. As I sat at a bar near the band with the other officers, Captain Donovan pushed a bottle of whiskey over and said, "Relax, Bray, have a drink."

I poured a glass, and another, and another. The next thing I knew I was on the stage dancing with one of the showgirls. I hadn't wanted to go. I had no idea how to dance. With the encouragement of the whiskey, and the prodding of the other officers and my platoon, I climbed on the stage and made a fool of myself.

Captain Donovan and the other officers paid for their fun later that night. I passed out in the BOQ (bachelor officers' quarters) and threw up all over the place. They cleaned up the mess, and, amid great laughter the next morning, told me all about it.

The incident did help to cement the bond between my platoon and me. For weeks, I heard remarks about my drinking and dancing abilities—though the comments were always made in a respectful manner. I don't think I could have gotten a better platoon if I had handpicked the men from all the soldiers in Vietnam.

I spent the remainder of the stand down nursing a hangover. I walked over to the PX and bought a carton of cigarettes. I had never smoked in my life. C rations in the field came with a chocolate bar and a little package of four cigarettes. I started smoking them and acquired the habit. I often wondered if the tobacco companies provided them free to the government to get us hooked.

We checked out our weapons and flew back to LZ Liz. The second afternoon we were there, I was sitting in the command bunker, writing a letter home, when one of the men ran in and said bunker four had caved in. It had been raining all day. I ran down to the bunker and the whole side and part of the roof had fallen in. The men were milling around outside, and Doc Miles was treating Pfc. Buddy Quong's leg. I asked if anyone was still inside.

"No, they got everyone out," Doc Miles said.

No one seemed to be hurt aside from the man with the injured leg. Willy Lewis stood nearby, holding his side. I asked him if he was all right.

"Yeah, one of the beams hit me while I was lying on my bunk, but it didn't hurt much," he said. He complained that the fallen sandbags had ruined the new tape recorder he had just bought at Chu Lai. He continued to hold his side, but kept insisting that it didn't hurt badly.

"I'm going to call a Dust Off and have you checked out anyway," I told Lewis.

"Make sure you get my tapes out of there, sir, and put 'em in a plastic bag," he said as he walked toward the helipad with Doc Miles. A Dust Off arrived from Bronco and took Lewis and Quong back to the brigade aid station. We got all the gear and Lewis's tapes out of the collapsed bunker and moved them to another.

Back at the command bunker, I finished my letter. An hour later, I called Top at Bronco to check on Lewis and Quong.

"I just got the word, sir. Lewis's dead. He died at the aid station from internal injuries."

I had a hard time believing he was dead. He had stood on the LZ laughing and joking with Miles while they waited for the Dust Off. We gathered his personal belongings and shipped them to the rear. I put his tapes in a plastic bag and sealed it shut.

The next morning the battalion commander called a meeting at the site of the fallen bunker.

"I want this goddamned bunker rebuilt today," he yelled, standing on the collapsed sandbags. "That means sergeants and officers,
too." He turned and climbed back up the hill to his command
bunker, leaving us standing there.

One of the other lieutenants turned to me and said, "Hell, we
didn't build the thing in the first place. The engineers did."

"No," I said, "but it looks like we get to rebuild it."

We spent the rest of the day tearing down and rebuilding the
bunker that had killed Lewis. Captain Donovan helped fill sandbags.
It was only my second meeting with the battalion commander, and
my impression of him was getting worse.

Ambush along the River

The third night we were on LZ Liz, the radar station on the South Observation Post detected enemy movement south of us along the Tra Cau River. Artillery fire missions were directed at the targets, but the next night movement was picked up again in the same area. The following day, Captain Donovan ordered me to conduct an ambush along the river that night. I told Sergeant Eddy to have his squad ready to move out at 1800 hours. Ten men would be on the snake—Stub, Doc Miles, Sergeant Eddy, his six-man squad, and me.

After carefully studying my map of the terrain along the river, I selected a site for the ambush near the remains of an old railroad bridge that had once spanned the river. Several trails converged near the destroyed bridge. In order for the Viet Cong or North Vietnamese Army to move back and forth from the coastal villages to the safety of the jungle some three kilometers west of the bridge, they would have to use one of the trails that paralleled the river. The thick underbrush and dense bamboo thickets surrounding the river would serve to funnel enemy movement toward the ambush site and provide excellent cover for our trek to the location.

After I briefed the members of the ambush team and reported our location for the night to battalion headquarters, we loaded our gear and made our way south out of LZ Liz at dusk. We traveled light, just taking the radio, weapons, and water. We left our heavy rucksacks in the bunkers. The afternoon's rain had slowed to a light drizzle with a heavy cloud cover. I hoped it would stop. I didn't look forward to lying motionless all night in a heavy rain. Before we left the landing zone, I grabbed a starlight scope in case the cloud cover lifted.

We made our way south to a location about five hundred meters north of the ambush site, utilizing the hedgerows and brush for cover. I informed the men that this would be our rendezvous point if anything went wrong or if any of us became separated. Because it was on the railroad bed, it would be an easy place to find in the dark.

Under the cover of darkness, we moved to the ambush site. I selected a spot on the railroad bed forty meters from where a trail emerged from the brush and crossed the railroad berm. The part of the berm where we would hide had been washed out by heavy rains in the past and provided us with ideal concealment and cover. I placed two claymore mines on the berm facing the intersection of it and the trail, ran the electrical wire back to the washed-out spot, and connected the handheld detonators. I positioned two men a few meters to our rear and had them deploy claymores to protect our flanks and rear from the approach of enemy from that direction. The other men faced the trail. We lay silent and waited.

I glanced down at my watch—0215 hours. Stub had just sent the hourly situation report back to battalion by breaking "squelch" on the radio two times, the prearranged signal that all was okay on the ambush. The drizzle stopped, but we were soaking wet. I pulled my nylon poncho liner up over my shoulders. We couldn't use our ponchos. They made too much noise when we moved them. I picked up the starlight scope and flipped on the switch. Looking through the lens down the berm, I saw only a green luminous background with green sparkles. The scope was useless with the heavy cloud cover.

My sense of awareness to my surroundings became incredibly acute. Every sound was amplified a hundred times. I was aware of the

sound of my heart beating. I could hear droplets of water falling
from the bamboo leaves twenty feet away. The slightest movement
from one of my men could be heard for a mile, it seemed to me.

I heard a sound in the dark, like two limbs brushing together. I
turned my head to the side, straining to listen. Nothing but the
sound of water droplets and the humming of mosquitoes. I stared
into the darkness along the berm and saw the outline of what
appeared to be a man standing on the edge of a bamboo thicket. I
tried looking off to the side of the object as I had been taught in
training. If I stared directly at the object in the dark, it would disappear and change shape. My heart began to beat faster. I could tell
from the alertness of the man lying beside me that he had heard the
noise also.

The shape remained motionless. Perhaps, I told myself, it was only
a bush I had failed to notice earlier. I nearly talked myself into that
explanation when suddenly I saw the unmistakable movement of the
object and heard the crunching sound of gravel as the man took a
step into the open. No movement of civilian personnel was allowed
in Vietnam after dark. Only the enemy moved in the dark. I had told
the men in the ambush not to fire until I gave the signal—the deto-
nation of the claymore mines aimed at the trail crossing. I held the
detonators, one in each hand, and waited. He had to be the point
man for a larger group behind him. He would surely check out the
crossing and signal the others to follow. I would wait until they were
in the kill zone of the claymores before I squeezed the detonators.

The seconds seemed like hours as the man slowly ascended the
side of the berm. I expected him to continue across the berm following the trail when suddenly he turned and began walking directly
toward our position. There was no sign of anyone accompanying
him. He continued to advance, unaware of our presence. Forty
meters, thirty meters. I gently laid down the claymore detonators
and placed my hands around the stock grip and forearm of my M-
14. Twenty meters. I raised the M-14 and pointed it directly at the

center of the man's chest. In one continuous movement, I flipped off the safety with my forefinger and squeezed the trigger twice. There was a deafening roar as the other men of the ambush fired almost simultaneously with my shots. The man was thrown backward and fell as if he were a rag doll.

"Don't shoot, GI. Don't shoot, GI," a shrill, high-pitched voice said.

O'Doud and Smith's M-60 fired a long burst down the berm, and Armstrong's shotgun roared. The body in front of us was still. Then silence. The firing had lasted only five or ten seconds, yet it had shattered the life of the person lying in front of us. For the remainder of my life, I could never say that I hadn't killed another human being.

We lay in silence for the next few minutes, watching and listening for any sight or sound of further enemy presence. When none came, I called the duty officer on Liz and informed him that we had blown our ambush, the results of which were one Viet Cong killed in action. I then informed him that we were going to move our position one hundred meters to the north. I quickly assembled the men and redeployed the ambush in the new position. The clouds had broken up, and occasionally a bright half-moon shined through. When it did, in the distance we could see the person we had killed.

As we lay in our new position, I kept going over and over the event that had just occurred. What puzzled me most was the exclamation I had heard over the gunfire—"Don't shoot, GI. Don't shoot, GI"— repeated twice in that high-pitched, terrified voice. The explanation for the timbre of the voice would become startlingly clear at dawn, when many new images would be added to my memory.

As I approached the motionless body in the early morning light, I felt a sense of pride, remembering my uncle's stories. As the stories had recounted, this was the enemy, and we had killed him. What his stories had not included was a description of the aftermath of death. The first image that became ingrained in me as I neared the corpse was the blood. I hadn't known that the human body contained so much blood. The gravel behind the body was painted a deep red for many feet. Small rivulets had run several directions from the body to form red pools in the depressions on the side of the berm. It is difficult to describe the odor of torn flesh and blood, but it was a sweet, musty smell like no other I had ever experienced. A smell I would come to know well over the next year.

The body lay on its side, facing us, with an arm stretched outward, covering its face. The black silk pajamas were blood-soaked. As I came near the body, careful not to step in the red pools, I saw several small, uniformly round holes in the clothing that had been made by the bullets as they found their mark, one directly in the center of the chest. One of my men kicked the outstretched arm covering the face, and as it fell away, the question of why a high-pitched voice had rung out was answered. It was a woman.

At the time, I don't know why I was surprised to discover that the first person I had killed was a woman. After all, I had often heard the tale of my uncle being shot by a female. Perhaps it was that all my life I had been taught never to hurt a girl. Or maybe it was simply the thought of all the years my mother had spent loving and caring for me as a child. Still, that I had killed this woman didn't bother me then as much as it would come to bother me over the next thirty years.

As I walked around the woman's body, I found that there was no neatness in violent death. Despite the small, uniform, round holes in the front of her body, the 150-grain bullets had literally torn away her back. Great blobs of flesh and internal organs protruded from the gaping exit wounds the bullets had made. Armstrong's shotgun blast had ripped the back of the woman's head away. I only looked for a second, but it was enough to last a lifetime.

A small green canvas bag lay next to the woman. She wasn't carrying a weapon. One of the men passed the bag to me, and upon opening it, I discovered several glass vials containing what appeared to be medicine, several rolls of bandages made from strips of cloth,

and a syringe and needle. I assumed she was likely a nurse returning
from treating wounded enemy soldiers in the jungle. A plastic Vietnamese identification card with the dead woman's photograph on
it was also in the bag.

"Man, we wasted her," one of the men standing around the body
said.

"Some VC just lost his boom-boom girl," said another.

They had grown used to seeing someone die a violent death. In
the still-recent past, members of their own platoon had suffered the
same fate.

As I stood over the body, absorbing the details of the woman's
waxen facial features and unseeing, deep-brown eyes, which were
fixed straight ahead of her, I felt no remorse or sorrow for my
involvement in her death.

We prepared to return to LZ Liz. I called the battalion headquarters and requested instructions on how to dispose of the body.
I didn't know if we were supposed to bury the woman or call for a
helicopter to remove her back to one of the bases in the rear. The
officer on duty informed me we were to leave her where she was, that
the local villagers would take care of her body. When we left LZ Liz
three days later to begin our three weeks of operations in the field,
I led my platoon near the spot where the ambush had taken place.
There, on top of the berm, lay the body of the woman we had killed,
barely recognizable.

CHAPTER 9

Jungle Duty and the 515 Valley

This time when we left Liz there were no helicopters. We did what infantrymen had done forever—we walked. It would be the last time for three weeks that my boots were dry. Before we reached fifty meters from the perimeter, we were sloshing in ankle-deep water. The company moved south along the east side of the South OP. Our objective for the day was to cross the Tra Cau and to establish a night defensive position close to where a small stream entered the river— near the area where the radar had picked up movement for the last three nights and where we had killed the Viet Cong nurse.

Our first night there, the reason for the increased enemy activity became apparent. VC and North Vietnamese Army sappers (Viet Cong infiltrators) hit LZ Bronco. Some of them got through the wire with their satchel charges—explosives carried in a canvas bag—and destroyed artillery pieces and bunkers. In the village of Duc Pho, adjacent to Bronco, the Viet Cong burned several of the hooches and small Vietnamese businesses along Highway 1. Many of the villagers worked inside Bronco during the day as laborers and house girls for the Americans. Some of them paid for the association with their lives. The next morning, my platoon would patrol to the west and then move south in an attempt to intercept any of the Viet Cong or NVA retreating to the mountains after their attack on Bronco and Duc Pho.

The morning was foggy, and a light rain fell. To the west, the mountains were shrouded from view by a thick bank of low, gray clouds. We had moved only a few hundred meters when the point man approached a small ditch, barely four feet wide, to wade across. We had already crossed several ditches, wading up to our knees. As he stepped into the water, he disappeared. Several of us ran to the edge. I was stripping off my rucksack and pistol belt to jump in after him when he bobbed to the surface a few feet downstream. We grabbed him by the straps on his pack and pulled him onto the muddy bank. He coughed and rolled onto his stomach, blowing water from his nose.

"Are you okay?" I asked, helping him to his feet.

"Damn, sir, I can't even swim, and I didn't think I was ever going to come back to the top. I dropped my rifle and helmet."

We spent fifteen minutes diving in the ten-foot-deep water before we retrieved his M-16 and helmet.

His squad leader asked him if he wanted someone else to walk point. "Hell no, I'm point," he replied.

We got our gear on and prepared to resume the patrol. The point man found a nearby stand of bamboo and cut a long slender pole with the squad leader's machete. I never saw him step off into water again without testing its depth.

As we turned to the south, the open terrain allowed movement in a wedge formation, with the center squad slightly forward. I preferred this formation when the ground was open because it gave me better control over the platoon. I could see all three squad leaders, and they could see me. The platoon was down to twenty-two men, counting Stub and me. I had received a few replacements, but several members of the platoon had completed their one-year tour of duty and gone home. I envied them. I had ten months to go.

As we continued southward, we heard the sound of gunfire to our southeast—at first it was only a few long bursts of automatic rifle fire, but it quickly swelled to the sound of a firefight with machine gun fire and rocket explosions. Third Platoon was operating in that direction. I listened to the calls passing back and forth between Third Platoon and Captain Donovan. They had flushed a group of five or six Viet Cong from a small village as they approached it. The Viet Cong had fired at them for a minute and then evaded to the west. Third Platoon had killed one of the VC and captured an AK-47 rifle.

The captain called the battalion headquarters and requested helicopter gunships. He then called me and told me to move my platoon quickly to the south and to set up an ambush in the hopes of catching the fleeing VC. I moved the platoon to a large ditch that ran north and south and positioned the men along a one-hundred-meter front facing east. We were about seven or eight hundred meters west of Third Platoon. The firing to the east had stopped. In the distance toward Bronco, we could hear the loudening sound of rotor blades as helicopters approached. The Sharks searched the area for more than an hour with no results.

After the gunships departed, Third Platoon and Second Platoon made a sweep west to our position. They found a trail of blood leading out of the village but lost it after a short distance. The VC had escaped, probably to the south and the mountains. I thought of the female nurse we had killed and wondered how many more like her had made the deadly trip into the mountains to treat the wounded of the Viet Cong and NVA. After we established a day laager, I went over to the command post and looked at the AK-47 that had been captured. It looked new, with no scratches on the stock, and none of the bluing was worn on the metal. It was the first AK I had ever held. I removed the magazine and looked at the ammunition. The bullets seemed short and stocky compared to the rounds for my M-14. They looked much larger when compared to the 5.56 mm rounds of the M-16.

We continued our daily ritual of patrols and ambushes. We had been in the field for close to a week. Each day we moved closer to the mountains in the west. At times they weren't visible through the mist, but when the clouds thinned and the sun burned away the fog, they towered over us.

Battalion headquarters wanted the number of nightly ambushes increased. The company sent out as many as nine per night. I took one of them on the south bank of the Tra Cau, just across from the South OP. That night one of my squads and I learned the meaning of friendly fire.

We moved fifteen hundred meters to reach our snake location. The rain carried with it the usual cold winds off the mountains. With each step we took, the red mud stuck to our boots until we felt like we were dragging weights around on our feet. The closer we pushed toward the river, the thicker the brush became. I wasn't looking forward to spending another night near the water with the mosquitoes. I hoped the cold wind would thin them down some.

We approached the area where I wanted to set up the snake. Rather than taking all the men to search for a good site in the area, I decided to take Stub and one other man ahead. We moved a hundred meters forward and stopped behind a large tree. I spotted a good position for the ambush just ahead where a large ditch ran into the river. A trail coming from the direction of Bronco crossed a small clearing near the ditch. We moved back to where the rest of the men waited in the brush. Darkness was fast approaching, and in a few minutes, visibility would be next to nothing. We set out claymores facing up and down the trail.

It was an excellent ambush site. Over the years, rains had washed the ditch out to a depth of about four feet. If we knelt in the flat, muddy bottom, only our heads and shoulders would be exposed. The river behind us protected our flanks and rear. I called our position into battalion and settled into the ditch for a long night.

Surely nothing would move on a night like this, I thought. We could barely see our hands in front of our faces. It began to rain harder, and the water ran two inches deep in the bottom of the ditch. I whispered to the men that we would maintain 50 percent alert until 0400, then 100 percent until dawn. Every other man settled down into the ditch, leaning back on the sloped bank with his poncho liner wrapped over his head to try and sleep. I told Stub I would take the first three hours. He pulled the radio off his back and laid it on the bank beside me. He slid down toward the bottom of the ditch and curled up on his side under his poncho liner.

It grew darker still. Usually at night we could see a light from one of the firebases or even a flare shot into the air for illumination. Not that night. We couldn't even see the horizon over the bamboo thickets. It was one solid curtain of blackness.

Two times I heard the speaker on the radio whisper "Charlie four-four sit-rep, over." Each time I pushed the talk button twice to break squelch. I could hear noises in the brush across the clearing some thirty meters away. I shook Stub, and out of the blackness came the sound of a pig grunting. The noise became louder, mingled with the sound of thrashing in the bamboo thicket. Two boars were fighting. The thrashing and grunting continued for a few minutes until one of the pigs squealed and ran away through the brush. I couldn't see a thing.

It wasn't unusual to see pigs in the valley. Over the years they had escaped from the villagers and turned wild to live in the mountains. At night they came down into the valley to dig up roots with their snouts. I had noticed on several occasions while on patrol that the ground around some of the bamboo thickets looked as if a huge spade had churned it up. One night while I was lying in an ambush near the old 515 road, two of the largest pigs I had ever seen walked casually down a trail through our kill zone. One of them had tusks that were easily ten inches long extending out of his lower jaw. We had let them continue on their way.

The rain slowed to a fine mist. I looked at my watch: 2050 hours. I would wake Stub in ten minutes after the hourly sit-rep. The rain had washed the insect repellant off my arms and mosquitoes were biting me. I reached up to my helmet to get the bottle of repellant out of the elastic band. Swish-BOOM-BOOM-BOOM. A blinding flash of light and the loudest explosions I had ever heard erupted around me. The concussion threw me back, sprawled over Stub in the bottom of the ditch. Huge chunks of mud and debris rained down on us. I scrambled to crawl out of the bottom. The smell of burned powder filled the air. I crawled back over Stub, looking for the radio. The concussion and shaking of the ground had caused it to slide to the bottom of the ditch. I found the handset and pushed the button.

"Cease fire, cease fire, you're firing on friendlies!" I yelled into the handset.

"Use proper radio procedure," came a calm voice over the speaker.

"Goddamn it, you're firing artillery on us!" I yelled back.

There was a long silence on the radio.

"Anybody hurt?" I asked, looking at the men down the ditch. They held their weapons, crouching in the bottom.

"I don't think so," said a voice. It was still so dark I couldn't see all the men. I told Stub to check everyone to make sure they weren't hit. The artillery fire stopped. I had known from the sound that it made before it impacted that it was artillery—which the VC and NVA did not have.

"Artillery is check fired," said a voice over the radio.

I calmed down. "Zulu two-one, this is Charlie four-four; we just had three rounds of artillery dropped right on top of our position, over," I said into the handset.

In a few seconds, the voice came back asking for the grid coordinates of our position. I slid to the bottom of the ditch and pulled out my map. Using my flashlight with the red lens, I repeated the grid coordinates of our position that I had written with grease pencil on the map.

A few seconds later, the voice replied, "We don't have anybody on our map at that location."

My anger rose again. "Zulu two-one, that's the position I called in at 1800 hours, confirmation initials Bravo Whiskey." It was standard procedure to ask for the initials of the person taking your message when calling in positions or other important information.

Stub informed me that all the men were okay, except for some ringing in the ears.

A different voice came over the radio. "Charlie four-four, we've got your location and will check to see what happened. All your people okay?"

I confirmed that we were and repeated the coordinates of our location. When I asked for his initials, he paused and said, "Bravo Whiskey."

We spent the remainder of the night huddled in the ditch waiting for dawn. None of the men went back to sleep. When daylight came, I saw how close we had all come to dying. Twenty feet in front of the ditch, a crater four feet in diameter marked the impact of one of the artillery rounds. A few meters over from the ditch, two more showed how close they had hit. I learned one thing that night: the artillery fire from LZ Bronco was highly accurate. The firers had triangled us perfectly. Had we been lying in the brush instead of the ditch, few, if any of us, would have survived.

When we returned to the company NDP, Captain Donovan explained what had happened. When I called in the location for the ambush, the duty officer failed to mark our position on the fire control map for the artillery. The radar unit on top of the South OP had detected movement at our site and called a fire mission on the suspected enemy location. When I told the captain that we hadn't been moving around at our ambush site, I remembered the herd of pigs nearby. I wondered how many of the recent enemy movements reported by radar had been nothing more than animals moving along the river.

Day by day, the company continued to move west toward the mountains. One morning, Captain Donovan assigned my platoon a patrol that would take us deep into the jungle. We had spent the night in the waist-high elephant grass covering the foothills. At one time the area had been jungle, but it had been sprayed with herbicide in a north-south flight pattern. An abrupt transition from elephant grass to the jungle had resulted. From the grassland I could easily see the layers of the triple-canopy jungle. A mass of vines and creepers covered the lower ground level. The middle layer was composed of intermediate-sized trees, filled with the leaves of the vines that ran down the tree trunks and hung from the branches to the jungle floor. Giant hardwoods towered above everything else, reaching more than a hundred feet into the air.

The plan called for my platoon to enter the jungle and to go forward for one kilometer, then to turn south and link up with the rest of the company, which would be spread out behind a small stream called Ba Kahn on my map. We would give the company two hours to get into position before we moved out.

When I showed Sergeant Knowles our route, he shook his head and said, "The last time we went into a place like that, we lost seven guys."

When the two hours were up, I radioed the captain, who told me the company was in position and that we should move out. We started the five-hundred-meter walk through the elephant grass to the edge of the jungle in single file. As the point man approached the green curtain of vegetation, I saw him jump suddenly sideways. He stared into the grass. I moved forward, signaling the men to halt and face outward for security. When I reached the point man's position, I saw what had startled him. A human skull lay facing upward, surrounded by scattered bones. The lower jaw drooped from the skull, exposing rows of white teeth. In the side of the skull, a one-inch triangular hole gave evidence to what had killed the man. Where the round had exited on the opposite side was a hole big enough to put a fist through. Nearby lay the rotting remains of an empty canvas bag and a pith helmet like those worn by the NVA. Pigs had rooted the ground around the bones and chewed on some of the remains. We searched the area for a weapon but found nothing. From the looks of the head wound, the NVA soldier had been killed by artillery fire.

The rain started up again, and we moved into the jungle. It was like stepping into a cave. Our eyes slowly adjusted to the gloom under the canopy. One of the men near the front of the column stopped and pointed upward with his rifle. I followed the direction of his rifle into the trees and spotted the bottom of a bamboo platform lashed between two limbs in one of the hardwoods. The limbs that had been cut and placed around the platform for screening had turned brown; otherwise we probably wouldn't have spotted it. From the platform, an enemy soldier would have a clear view of the valley below.

Huge droplets of water fell from the leaves overhead, making a thudding sound as they hit the jungle floor. When they hit a leaf or vine near us, we were sprayed with a fine mist of water. The smell of rotting wood filled the air. Nothing remained on the jungle floor for long. The constant dampness quickly turned it back to soil. I had trained a week in the jungles of Panama, but nothing compared to this. There wasn't a hint of sunlight as we slowly moved deeper into the gloom.

After we walked a few hundred meters, the creepers and lower vegetation became less dense. Visibility went from a few meters to as far as fifty meters in places. We continued forward in single file. I put flankers out forty meters on each side of the point and instructed them to keep sight of the column.

We moved slowly west until we came to the north base of a large hill. At that point, we were to turn south and travel two kilometers over the hill to link up with the rest of the company. The hill had no name on the map, just the number sixty-four, indicating its height above sea level in meters. We started up the slope of the hill. At first, we climbed with ease, but quickly the slope became steeper, and at times the only way we made headway was to grab the vines or roots and to pull ourselves up. The vegetation had grown thicker, and the flankers moved to within twenty meters of the point to maintain visual contact. After an hour, we reached a small plateau halfway up the hill. I called a rest break and radioed the captain to give him our location. He advised me to move slowly and keep alert. The advice wasn't necessary. I hated the jungle. I could imagine the North Vietnamese Army behind every bush or rock.

I dropped my pack beside Stub and leaned back on my elbow to rest a few minutes. Some of the men opened C rations. Others drank from their canteens. I was about to ask Stub a question about the radio when something screamed loudly over our heads. We both jumped and reached for our weapons. Another scream followed, joined by a chorus of howls and screeches. I looked up into the tall trees and saw a group of long-tailed monkeys scurrying through the branches. I laid my M-14 back across my pack and got my canteen out of its canvas holder on my pistol belt.

Sergeant Knowles sat a few feet away, smiling at my reaction to the sound of the monkeys. "They spooked me too, sir, but that was funny," he said.

I watched the monkeys making their way down the side of the hill through the treetops. "I wonder if they're VC or NVA?" I said.

He grinned and looked out at the monkeys. "Definitely VC. Didn't you hear 'em saying 'no VC, no VC' as they ran away?"

I raised the canteen to get a drink of water.

"Sir, look at the back of your arm," Stub said.

I grabbed my elbow and pulled the skin around. A three-inch leaf appeared to be stuck to my arm. I brushed it with my hand and realized it wasn't a leaf. It was a leach! Stub put a cigarette to its back, and it curled up and fell to the ground. I picked up my rifle and smashed it with the stock. Blood splattered onto the leaves nearby. A small stream of blood ran down my arm from where the leach had been attached.

"You can't even feel the little bastards biting you," I said and stood to wash the blood off my arm with water from my canteen. I didn't sit back down on the damp leaves.

We moved out and continued up the hill. I arranged the men in two parallel columns twenty meters apart with flankers to the side. I warned the point men to go slowly. I didn't want to walk into another ambush like the one that had occurred directly north of us a couple of months back.

We neared the top of the hill. Water continued to drip from the canopy overhead. My map showed a small saddle running north and south on the top. As we approached the highest point of the hill, the point man on the left dropped to one knee and signaled me forward. I gave a palm-down signal to the rest of the platoon, indicating the men should stop and face outward for security. I crouched low and approached the point man. He pointed to a small patch of brush twenty meters ahead. Looking closely through the shadows, I could see the dark opening of a hole in the ground.

I motioned Embree forward and whispered for him to take two men and to crawl around to the left to check out the hole. I moved an M-60 team near the point to cover the men. I watched as they moved to the rear of the opening. Embree motioned me forward. As I crawled toward his location, I detected a faint odor reminiscent of the smells in a Vietnamese village. When I reached his position, I could see the back entrance to a camouflaged bunker. I crawled up to the opening and looked inside. It was empty.

I signaled the men forward. The vegetation opened considerably in the saddle, so we could see for close to seventy-five meters. Forty meters from the first bunker, we found another, and then another. I called the commanding officer and told him what we had found. We were seven or eight hundred meters north of their blocking position. Overhead, I could hear the sound of rotor blades. The CO told us to continue checking out the area.

We moved slowly around the saddle. By the time we finished our search, we had found more than twenty bunkers. Some of them were large enough to hold as many as eight to ten men. Whoever had used them had been there for quite some time. Small trails led from bunker to bunker. Communication wire was buried between them as well. Inside, we discovered folded and discarded banana leaves that had been used to carry cooked rice. In one bunker, the imprint of tripod legs showed the employment of a crew-served weapon, either a heavy machine gun or a recoilless rifle. Outside, some of the vegetation used to camouflage the bunkers had barely begun to wilt.

Sergeant Knowles walked over to where I was checking out a large bunker near the center of the saddle. "It's a good thing for us they pulled out last night," he said.

Knowles was right. Even if we had taken out the first bunker we had encountered, once we reached the crest of the hill we would have come under the fire of four or five of the bunkers near it. Whoever had laid out this defensive position had used the ground well. The bunker with the crew-served weapon could provide supporting fire for at least eight of the others.

One of the men on perimeter security discovered a row of fighting positions one hundred meters down the slope to the east of the saddle. Overhead, in the tallest trees, we found three observation platforms that would have given the NVA an excellent view of the valley. They had been observing us for the last week. When we started moving toward the mountains, their commander had made the decision to retreat farther into the jungle rather than to stand and fight. I agreed with Knowles. I was glad they had left.

I called Captain Donovan and asked him if he wanted me to start destroying the bunkers with explosives. I was eager to get off the hill and to rejoin the company. His reply was not what I expected. He told me that after we left the area, they were going to call a fire mission on the saddle using the big eight-inch guns on Bronco. As for my platoon, the battalion CO, Price, wanted us to move west one kilometer to see if we could make contact with the retreating NVA. The rest of the company would maintain its blocking position along the small stream. I could hardly believe the order. He wanted me to go chasing after a reinforced company of NVA with only twenty-two men. Although I couldn't see him overhead, I could still hear the rotor blades of the command-and-control helicopter.

After I assembled the men, we started west down the steep slope. As the vegetation grew thicker, we could only move in a single file. If we sent a flanker out, he would be lost from sight in ten meters. Again, I cautioned the point man to move slowly.

The gloom under the jungle canopy brightened, and the big droplets of water ceased to fall. The rain had stopped. As we progressed down the slope, I thought of the stories I had heard from the tactics instructors at Fort Benning about the platoon that had been cut off from the rest of its unit in the Ia Drang Valley several years earlier. The soldiers had moved off in search of the NVA and become surrounded. By the time the rest of the unit reached them the next day, they had been annihilated. Among the first to die had been the platoon leader and the squad leaders.

After moving west for five hundred meters, we broke out of the jungle and entered a large area of waist-high elephant grass. It took our eyes several minutes to adjust to the sudden change of brightness. Overhead I could see the C-and-C chopper making large circles high in the air. The CO wanted us to move southwest to check out trails in the elephant grass. I wondered why he couldn't fly lower in his helicopter and check them out from the air. Then I remembered the rumors that had been circulating around the battalion, that during a recent firefight involving Bravo Company, his C-and-C ship had supposedly been shot down by friendly fire. Maybe he didn't trust his own men anymore.

We headed southwest and soon came across a fresh trail tromped through the elephant grass. The crumpled green grass indicated that the path was recently made. The trail ran from the direction of the hilltop base camp and led toward the high mountains to the west. That was out of our area of operations. If the NVA soldiers had fled in that direction, it would be some other battalion's job to find them. We turned southeast and joined the rest of the company. The C-and-C ship disappeared to the north toward Liz.

"Glad to see you, lieutenant," the captain said as I found his position along the stream.

"Not nearly as glad as I am," I replied.

The company moved out of the mountains and, over the next several days, worked its way up the valley to a position directly west of Liz, killing two VC and losing several men to booby traps along the way. We were in a day laager position when a supply helicopter arrived carrying a CBS News camera crew. They had traveled there to interview members of Charlie Company about the My Lai massacre. News of the killings had recently been made public in the United States. A few men who had been with the company during the massacre were in the rear at LZ Bronco. They had been picked up by army investigators and flown back to the United States. The replacements who joined the company told of pictures on the television back home of piles of dead women and children around the village. Murder charges were being filed against Lieutenant Calley, the former leader of my platoon. I heard the reporter saying things like "murder," "atrocities," and "massacre." I didn't give it much thought. I knew I wasn't capable of shooting down women and children in cold blood. My hatred for these people wasn't nearly at that level.

I prepared to take my platoon on a patrol through the villages east of the company position. As we were moving out, I noticed a cameraman standing to the side with his camera on his shoulder pointed toward us. The reporter standing nearby asked me if I would have the men fire their weapons into the brush. I ignored him and continued on the patrol.

We finished our three weeks in the field and returned to Liz. The week in the dry bunkers passed quickly. While we were there, the higher-ups decided to make the 515 Valley a free-fire zone. They had already started doing the same to the Gaza Strip. While we were on Liz, near the Strip, Alpha Company found one of the largest rice caches that had ever been found in Vietnam. The local villagers swore they knew nothing about the rice and had no knowledge of the VC or NVA. The rice was airlifted to some of the pacified villages, though it likely ended up in the stomach of the local Viet Cong or NVA in the mountains. The pacified villages were full of Viet Cong sympathizers.

We marched off Liz at dawn, separated into platoon-size units. My platoon was responsible for clearing the center of the 515 Valley. The Vietnamese had no idea why we were coming. The first village we arrived at consisted of eight or ten hooches filled with old men, women, and children. A Vietnamese interpreter had been assigned to my platoon. I told him to tell the people that we were going to move them to a village away from the Viet Cong. They could take only the things they could carry in their hands. When the interpreter told them this, some of the old men began to argue with him.

One of them approached me with his hands clasped under his chin, shaking his head from side to side, saying, "No VC, no VC." I had the interpreter explain to him that if the people returned to their village, they would be killed. No one was allowed in a free-fire zone, day or night. If a helicopter flying over the area spotted any movement, the soldiers on it were not bound by the rules of engagement that covered populated areas. There, the enemy had to show hostile intent by wearing a uniform or carrying a weapon. Now, in the valley and on the Strip, anything that moved was a target.

We gathered the villagers in a small clearing next to their settlement. They carried a few items in their hands—a small picture from the shrine in their home, clothes, cooking utensils, and a few rice mats. The women cried and wailed in Vietnamese. I couldn't understand what they were saying, but I understood the crying. Most of the old men had the sullen and defiant expression on their faces that I had seen so many times before when dealing with the peasants. I popped a smoke grenade and guided the giant Chinook helicopter into the small clearing. We loaded the people into the back of the helicopter. As the door rose, I saw a very old man sitting next to it inside. He stared expressionless at the village behind me. Tears ran down the old man's face. His eyes met mine as the door closed. The look of defiance on his face changed to a look of hatred in his eyes. I didn't care. My job was to clear out the valley. Someone else could worry about winning his heart and mind.

As the Chinook faded from sight back toward Highway 1, the interpreter met me near the village.

"All VC, many VC," he said, referring to the villagers we had just sent away.

"If they weren't, they are now," I said, continuing toward the little cluster of grass houses. He looked at me as if he didn't understand.

We moved through the empty village, setting the houses on fire. They burned slowly at first, but as the heat dried the damp grass roofs, they burned faster. The moisture in the roofs caused great white clouds of smoke to rise upward in the valley. To the north and south, I saw more columns of smoke rising. To the south, I heard the muffled explosions of Second Platoon blowing up family bunkers. When the fires died down, I rigged C-4 explosive charges in the three bunkers of the village we had just burned and blew them away. One of the men asked me what to do with the few pigs and chickens wandering around the area. I told him to leave them for the Army of the Republic of Vietnam and local militia, the Popular Forces. We hardly ever saw South Vietnamese soldiers in the field who weren't carrying some peasant's chickens by the legs back to their base camps. The most vivid image we had of our allies was that of a chicken thief.

We moved west to the next village and repeated the process. Third Platoon called an urgent Dust Off for two wounded men who had tripped a booby trap near one of the villages they were burning. By the time we took a break at noon, we had worked our way across most of the valley. Only a couple of small villages remained northeast of an old abandoned dirt airstrip.

While we ate our C rations, two mortar rounds landed in the brush five hundred meters to our south. Our activity hadn't gone unnoticed by the Viet Cong in the mountains above the valley. Captain Donovan and Third Platoon on the north side of the valley heard the mortars fire. Liz rewarded them with a twenty-minute artillery barrage, followed with an air strike by two F-4 Phantoms that dropped napalm and five-hundred-pound bombs. The mortars stopped.

By late afternoon, 515 Valley was empty. A thick layer of smoke hung above it. The charred, smoking remains of the hooches provided the only evidence of where the villages had once stood. In one day, an American rifle company had destroyed a valley that had been occupied for thousands of years by poor farmers who only wanted to be left alone to grow their rice and raise their families. When the farmers returned to the valley a few years later, the Communists would tell them where to rebuild their grass houses.

Moving the people out of the valley didn't stop the Viet Cong from coming back. If anything, 515 Valley and the Gaza Strip became more dangerous places to operate. The VC could lay more mines and set more booby traps than before because they didn't have to worry about their families being in the area.

We continued our routine of daily patrols near the mountains and nightly ambushes on the trails leading to the populated areas near Highway 1. The monsoon rains slowed to an occasional shower every few days. With relief from the constant rain came oppressive heat. A few hours of sun would send temperatures soaring above one hundred degrees.

One morning in early January the captain asked me if I would like to take my platoon to the north end of the Gaza Strip to provide security for some engineers who were building a road. Because that meant we would escape the nightly ambushes and daily patrols in the valley, as well as spend nights in a secure firebase, I happily accepted the assignment.

CHAPTER **10**

The Easy Job

The next morning we assembled our gear and humped our way back to LZ Liz, four kilometers away, leaving the rest of Charlie Company in 515 Valley. As we sat around on the east side of Liz, waiting for the trucks to pick us up, the men joked around, relieved to be out of the field.

When he heard of our new assignment and that we would spend the nights in a secure firebase without guard duty, Corporal Embree commented, "This would almost be like a job in the rear." I hoped he was right.

Two flatbed army trucks hauled us the ten kilometers up Highway 1 to LZ "Dragon." We arrived late in the afternoon, just as the engineers returned with the equipment from working on the road. We watched as they parked their dozers, loaders, and dump trucks in the compound. I found the lieutenant in charge and told him we were the unit he had requested to provide security while they built the road.

"I'm damned glad to see you," he said. "A couple of days ago, one of the truck drivers got a bullet through the windshield of his truck. It wasn't bad till we started getting close to the dry ground on the other side of the paddies. Come on up the hill, and I'll show you where your platoon can stay."

119

He turned and headed up the hill toward a group of bunkers, showing me the layout of LZ Dragon. The base was oval-shaped, about three hundred meters wide and eight hundred meters long, located three hundred meters west of Highway 1. Two defensive perimeters surrounded LZ Dragon—the outside line guarded by an ARVN unit and Popular Forces stationed there, and the interior perimeter for the American advisers attached to the ARVN unit.

"I suggest you and your men stay in the advisers' compound with us," the lieutenant said with a smile.

Apparently, he didn't have any more regard for the ARVN and PF soldiers than I did.

"At least if anything happens at night, they usually make enough noise to alert us," he said.

The next morning dawned bright and clear. It would be a hot day. Outside the gates of Dragon, the sounds of Vietnamese traffic drifted over from Highway 1. Scooters, buses, ox-drawn wagons, and strange looking three-wheeled vehicles mixed with bicycles moved up and down the road. We weren't used to so much activity. The people on the road seemed oblivious to the fact that a war was going on around them. They gave my heavily armed platoon little more than a curious glance as they passed us standing on the side of the road, waiting for the engineers. Three of the engineers carrying metal detectors crossed the highway and started down the dirt road they had been building, sweeping their machines from side to side as they checked for mines and booby traps. They wore earphones connected to the metal detectors. We followed them down the red dirt road some distance back.

Three thousand meters to the east, atop the highest ground in the area, lay the village of Nui Ong Do. Nui Ong Do would become part of a program implemented in Vietnam known as the Strategic Hamlet Initiative. Under the program, the South Vietnamese government officials and their American advisers selected villages they considered loyal to the south and provided them with free materials and equipment necessary to construct permanent housing within a defensive perimeter. The idea was to isolate the villagers from the Viet Cong and deny the VC use of the surrounding area as a base for supplies and logistical manpower.

Because of their liberal use of sheet metal, compliments of the U.S. Army, these villages appeared to be more like "tin cities" than rural Vietnamese settlements. Those of us who conducted operations in the vicinity of such villages simply regarded them as better places for the Viet Cong to stay before their next guerrilla attack. Most of the villagers we removed from 515 Valley were relocated in the new project. A footpath across the high ground and rice paddies provided the only access from the village back to Highway 1. Because the fortified village would contain several hundred people, government officials had decided to build the one-lane dirt access road.

The minesweeping team reached the end of the road and pronounced it clear. The engineers had completed the road eastward across the flooded rice paddies to within five hundred meters of the tree line, which marked the start of higher ground. Once they reached that point, they would no longer have to haul fill dirt from LZ Dragon.

At the east end of the road, we deployed into a wedge formation and waded into the knee-deep rice paddies, moving toward the tree line to secure it. Ahead, we could see Vietnamese civilians moving down the slope along the footpath, headed in our direction. They came from the fortified village on their way to the markets along the highway. We reached the tree line and moved to positions where we could cover the engineers. The country to the north was fairly open with good visibility for several hundred meters. To the south, the vegetation was much thicker. The area south of the village had a reputation for being one of the most heavily booby-trapped places in the battalion's area of operations. I took two of the squads and made a short patrol around a ridge to the south. We saw nothing and returned to the edge of the rice paddies. It was a comfortable day with nothing to do except watch the engineers haul dirt to the end of the road and spread it with their dozers. A group of small children came down the trail and mingled with the men, bumming food and candy.

We followed the same routine for three more days. On the second morning I called a Shark helicopter gunship from Bronco to cover our approach to the higher ground across the paddies. On the third morning a Helix forward air controller was working the Gaza Strip to the south and flew over for us as we crossed the open paddies. By now the road was only a couple hundred meters from the higher ground, and the last kilometer of the road would be built much faster than the first two kilometers since the engineers wouldn't have to haul dirt. The engineer lieutenant informed me that once the road was completed they were going to clear all the vegetation around the fortified village for a distance of five hundred meters. We would be there for at least two more weeks.

I didn't like the routine. It was too predictable. The last thing I wanted was to be forced to do the same thing over and over. I knew that as we left the security of LZ Dragon each morning, the Viet Cong observed us. If we became predictable in our movements and routines, he would make us pay. As he sat in his grass hut along Highway 1 when we passed, or rode his bicycle lazily down the road pretending to be on some farmer's errand, he watched us patiently. Did we do something stupid like walk down one of the paddy dikes? Did the men seek out the shade of the only stand of trees located within hundreds of meters of the road to escape the oppressive heat? He only needed us to make one mistake. He was in no hurry. This was his home. He had probably been born within sight of where we were building the road. The Viet Cong soldiers made it clear they had not lost interest in our presence—as we soon found out.

On the third morning, as was the case each morning, the engineers began their sweep of the road with their metal detectors, followed by my platoon. The dozers and trucks loaded with dirt trailed behind. During construction of the one-lane road, the engineers had widened it at one-hundred-meter intervals to allow trucks returning for a new load of dirt to be able to pull over and let the trucks loaded with dirt pass. The minesweepers were fifty meters from the end of the road. We sat on the side of the road, waiting for them to complete their sweep. John Smith and Ron Bunch sat on the last turnaround.

After the minesweepers declared the road free of mines, I got the men up and prepared to move east toward the tree line. We stepped aside to let one of the truck drivers pull over into the turnaround area so he could back to the end of the road and dump his load. As his front tire neared the edge of the turnaround, the earth under the front of the truck erupted and shot outward across the paddy. The blast forced me backward a step, and I watched as the truck stood on its tailgate and balanced there. I could see the driver sitting in his seat as though he were going to drive the truck straight into the air. The truck began to fall back to earth, slowly at first, and then accelerating rapidly as it approached the ground. It hit hard and bounced twice on its wheels. I ran to the driver's side door and opened it. Miraculously, the driver was still conscious and didn't appear to be seriously injured. I called an urgent Dust Off from Bronco and evacuated him. One of the dozers pushed the damaged truck aside, and work on the road resumed. Smith and Bunch were shaken for the remainder of the day. The mine had exploded exactly where they had been sitting.

That afternoon, the road reached the high ground out of the paddies. The engineers brought in two more dozers and began pushing the bamboo and underbrush away from the path of the road. I considered remaining at the end of the road that night to conduct an ambush after the morning's incident with the mine, but quickly concluded that all the Viet Cong would have to do was watch the engineers returning to Dragon to realize that we weren't with them. Instead, the next day I would have the engineers build a fortified

position on top of a small hill near the village. That way we wouldn't
have to make the trip each day back and forth to the landing zone.
Besides, the cramped bunkers in the compound weren't that comfortable. They were full of rats and smelled bad. I discussed it with the
engineers, and they agreed that they would just as soon stay near the
road, too. They could park their equipment and save the two and
one-half kilometer trip each day back to Dragon.

The next morning we ate our C rations and gathered our packs
and weapons to make our last trip down the dirt road following the
minesweepers. Our confidence in their ability to locate mines had
diminished considerably.

Because of the nearly constant flow of Vietnamese civilians from
the village down the path past us to Highway 1, I was aware that all
of our movements were under the constant scrutiny of the Viet
Cong. They knew we would have to occupy or at least check the area
south of where the road was being built. There, thick vegetation surrounded an elevated ridge that ran parallel to the road, making it an
ideal place for the Viet Cong to ambush or snipe at the engineers.
The thick underbrush surrounding the ridge extended for several
kilometers back to the south toward the Gaza Strip and would afford
the Viet Cong an easy escape route if they decided to ambush us. I
decided to take up positions along that ridge. We would leave the
road near the point where it reached dry land and patrol the area to
the south for about five hundred meters, then circle back and
approach the ridge from the rear. If any Viet Cong were on the
ridge, we would be coming up behind them.

We found evidence of Viet Cong presence almost immediately.
The ground along the south side of the ridge caved in at several
places, indicating the presence of abandoned tunnels. Signs
posted on some of the trails leading south warned of the presence
of booby traps. The Viet Cong would often mark areas where they
had deployed mines and booby traps to warn civilians to stay out of
an area. Sometimes the traps were there, and sometimes they

weren't. We simply assumed that all trails were mined and never used them.

As we approached the crest of the ridge from the south, the vegetation thinned. Shortly, we could see the bulldozers as they continued to work on the road. A cloud of dust and diesel smoke hung in the air above them. The position afforded a good view of the surrounding countryside. We would use it for the remainder of the day. I told Embree to take his squad fifty meters east to the crest of the ridge and to establish a position there. They could only occupy one position; his squad was down to four men, counting himself. I told the other squads to spread out westward along the ridge. Stub and I found a spot near the center of the platoon. The terrain was open enough that I could see the entire group from our position in the middle. I looked at my watch. It was nearly 1100 hours. Shortly after noon, the engineers would start building the defensive position where we would spend the night.

The day turned oppressively hot. By mid-afternoon, the temperature would be well over one hundred degrees. As we settled into our positions, I noticed a group of children making their way up to our location from the trail below. I gave their presence little thought. From the beginning of the road construction, they had come around during the day to watch the trucks and dozers and bum us for the sweets in our C rations. The engineers had chased them off several times for fear of running them over or pushing a tree down on one of them. I didn't know if they were orphans or simply turned loose during the day by their parents to fend for themselves. They spoke broken English, and I had talked to them on several occasions. One little boy I particularly liked we had given the nickname "Tom." His left foot, from the ankle down, had been maimed by an explosion while he helped his grandfather in the rice paddies. Almost without exception, we discovered when we talked to the children that some of their immediate family members had been killed or maimed by the war going on around them. Tom was no exception. He told me his father had been in the South Vietnamese army and had been killed somewhere near Saigon. When his father was killed, his mother left him in the care of his grandparents and moved to Da Nang to find work.

Tom had an honest hatred of the Viet Cong. Each time we met, his greeting was always "VC number ten, GI number one," which basically meant "VC the worst, GI the best." Although he was only a child of seven or eight, he told me something that I have never forgotten. During one of our conversations, I asked him if he wasn't scared to walk in the countryside with his friends, knowing that the Viet Cong were out there, along with their mines and booby traps.

"No, I'm not scared," he said. "Someday the VC will kill me just like my father and my uncle. Maybe someday I go to America."

I heard the sound of children's laughter coming from second squad's location. Corporal Embree was one of the kids' favorites. He was always happy to share his C rations with them, and on more than one occasion he had carried extra meals from the firebase to give to them. I glanced in Embree and Wade's direction and saw Tom and two other children, a little boy the same size as Tom and a little girl of maybe six who was holding her hands over her mouth to hide her missing teeth as she giggled. Embree and Wade removed their packs and searched them, I assumed, for food for the kids. Williams, a rifleman, sat on the ground, looking toward them. One of the men hollered something to one of the other positions about a game of spades. I picked up the handset of the radio to call in our position for the day to battalion headquarters when a huge explosion erupted at second squad's location.

My most vivid images of Vietnam followed.

From fifty meters away, the blast wave and sound arrived simultaneously. Even at that distance, the wind from the blast blew up dust around me. A small limb in the bush beside me fell to the ground, clipped cleanly by a piece of shrapnel. I ran toward the site of the explosion, with its familiar cloud of dark blue-gray smoke hanging in the air overhead.

The sight was devastating. I came upon the body of one of my men lying on his back. I had no way of recognizing who he was because his head had been blown off even with the top of his shoulders. I heard the sound of moaning a few yards to my left. It was Boyd Wade, the M-60 machine gunner. He lay on his back with his eyes open wide, looking in my direction. I ran to where he lay and knelt beside him. He tried to tell me something, but I couldn't make out what he was saying. I put my arm under his neck and lowered my head closer to his face to understand him. I thought I heard him say "lieutenant" and "hurts" before, with each beat of his heart, great gushes of blood began to pump out of his mouth. I watched him choke on his own blood. I turned him over on his stomach in an effort to get the blood out of his mouth and to my horror saw a gaping hole in the middle of his back. He died in the next few seconds.

I stood up and returned to the man whose head had been blown off to find out who he was. I didn't want to look at his upper body. After all these long years later, I can still picture the strange and terrible sight of the severed blood vessels, the bright white tendons, and raw flesh of where his head had been connected to his shoulders. We wore dog tags in our bootlaces as well as around our necks. I knelt at his feet and gently rotated the dog tag attached to his bootlaces. It was Embree. Doc Miles and Stub tended another of my men, Williams, a few feet from Embree's body. He had been hit by shrapnel and had severe burns. Doc tore away his shirt and applied field bandages to his wounds to stop the bleeding.

As I stood up from Embree's body, I saw the children. Little Tom lay halfway down the slope of a small ditch. The first thing I noticed about him was that half of his skull had been blown away. He was lying at an angle where the sun shone directly on the part of his head where his brain had been. The gleaming white of the bone on the inside of his skull looked as if it had been painted with the brightest white paint imaginable. It is an image frozen in my mind.

At the bottom of the ditch lay the body of the other little boy and the little girl. Both were covered with blood and a small bright red stream ran down the ditch away from their bodies. The little boy lay across the legs of the little girl. Both had holes in their upper bodies. The little girl's arm lay across her mouth as if she were still trying to hide her missing teeth. I saw her move and heard her moan softly. Doc Miles and a couple of the men went to the bottom of the ditch to work on the kids. I ran back to the radio and requested an urgent Dust Off for one U.S. wounded in action and two Vietnamese WIA children. After battalion confirmed the Dust Off, I informed them that we had two U.S. killed in actions and one Vietnamese child KIA. They confirmed a Dolphin was on the way to pick up the KIAs.

As we waited for the Dust Off helicopter to evacuate Williams and the two kids back to Bronco, the magnitude and horror of what had happened began to sink in. As I stood near Wade's body, I noticed a small saltwater evergreen tree a few feet from where the explosion had occurred. It was covered with small pieces of human brains. The sunlight glistened on the droplets of blood, and to this day the evergreen is etched in my memory as if it were a Christmas tree decorated with human remains.

The crater from the explosion was near Embree's body. From the size of the hole in the ground and the sound it had made, the explosion was likely caused by a 105 mm artillery shell the Viet Cong had found unexploded in one of the nearby fields. Embree, Wade, and the children had been sitting or standing directly over the mine when it exploded. Whether it was one of my men or one of the kids who had triggered the explosion, no one will ever know.

Two helicopters approached our position. The first had large red crosses painted on the fuselage. We quickly put Williams and the two kids aboard, and it lifted off for the flight back to Bronco and the aid station. The second helicopter circled and approached. We had carried Embree, Wade, and the little boy to a nearby clearing. The helicopter landed, and I walked over to the side door. A metal ammunition can sat in the middle of the floor, containing black plastic body bags.

No one's last memory of a person should be to see him disappear into one of those bags, yet that is how we said good-bye to our friends and fellow soldiers in Vietnam. We put Wade, Embree, and the little boy in body bags and loaded them on board the helicopter. I recall the two pilots of the helicopter staring straight ahead and never looking as we placed the bodies in the bags and loaded them. I wish I could have looked away.

After the helicopter took away the bodies, it was unusually quiet. The engineers had stopped working and sat in the shade of their equipment at the bottom of the hill. We remained on the ridge near the spot where the explosion had occurred, sitting or standing, each man reflecting on what had happened. Embree's little squad had been wiped out. Only one man remained.

I made my way down the side of the hill to where the engineers stood around one of the bulldozers. I found the lieutenant. He had come up the hill while we were evacuating the wounded and talked to one of the men. He told me he was sorry about the loss of my two men. I asked him if he would do me a favor.

"Just ask," he replied.

I told him I wanted his men to take the dozers up to the top of the hill and to level the place where my men had been killed. Within an hour, the top of the ridge was nothing but bare dirt. They filled in the ditch where the kids and been blown by the booby trap. I found the lieutenant later that afternoon and thanked him. I've never met a better man.

We moved to the east end of the ridge and the dozers quickly formed a triangular-shaped defensive position with five-foot-tall outside berms. Before dark, they brought in a combat engineer vehicle

(CEV). It was the size of a main battle tank with a twenty-four-inch infrared searchlight. With its big main gun and machine guns protecting the perimeter, we had no more trouble from the Viet Cong. The day after the booby trap exploded, we held a memorial service for Embree and Wade. Captain Donovan flew up for the service.

The remaining ten days of road construction were uneventful. The engineers finished the road and cleared the area surrounding the village. We rejoined the rest of Charlie Company. Our easy job was one I wished we had missed.

I had been in Vietnam for five months. I was twenty years old, and it seemed that I had spent all my life in this place and, with seven months remaining, that it would be where I spent the remainder of my days. The map I carried was covered with sites where someone had been killed or maimed. It was as though no other way of life had ever existed. Memories of what life had been like back in the States became more and more surreal. I became so immersed in the war that I began to think that this was all life would ever be—to keep from getting killed and to hunt down someone else to kill. Each day began with a plot hatched by one of my superior officers to outwit the enemy and kill him, the success or failure of the plan measured by the body count.

CHAPTER 11

A Series of Lines

Large maps of the area of operations (AO) covered the walls of the battalion command bunker where my superiors hatched out their plans to defeat the enemy. Shelves along the walls held the many radios used to communicate with the companies in the field, the artillery units, the forward air controllers, and other support units. Clipboards hung on the walls to keep a record of all the information that came into the battalion command post. Tables and benches ran down one of the walls where the colonel's staff sat and coordinated all of the battalion's activities. The most impressive thing about the bunker, however, wasn't all the equipment and maps, but the briefing area for the frequent visitors who wore stars on their collars.

A miniature stage had been constructed on the side of the bunker for the briefings, and it was complete with podium and seating for the visiting VIPs. Behind the podium hung a large map of the AO and a large plastic chart with many rows and columns filled with grease pencil markings. Each of the four companies of the battalion had its allotted space on the chart. There was a column for Alpha Company, one for Bravo Company, one for Charlie Company, one for Delta Company, and a smaller column for the Recon Platoon. One of the staff member's special jobs was to keep the chart updated so the colonel could brief the visiting generals on the body count.

Under each company's designation, the chart was divided into smaller columns to list that company's numerical success or failure during a particular month. The enemy was marked in red. A column, divided into each day of the month, listed the number of enemies killed in action (KIA), wounded in action (WIA), or captured. Opposite the red column was a blue column for friendly casualties, which contained the same column for killed in action or wounded in action. It was an impressive chart.

The chart man kept a running total. With all its red and blue numbers, the officers could tell at a glance how successful the battalion had been in the last month at killing the enemy. The kill ratio was easily computed. A briefing with high red numbers and low blue numbers brought smiles from the generals. A briefing with low red numbers and high blue numbers brought suggestions that perhaps the battalion wasn't being aggressive enough in its pursuit of the enemy. Such a briefing was usually followed by a combat assault or a trip into the mountains by one of the companies.

The thing I remember most about the chart is that it only contained numbers. There were no names posted in blue pencil, only numbers. A blue "1" under one of the companies' names was easy to accept, especially if directly opposite, in the red KIA column, there was a red "5." The generals had no use for such information as the kid's name, age, hometown, and next of kin. All this information was readily available, but it wasn't reflected on the chart.

I saw the chart after my platoon's assignment with the engineers. Listed under Charlie Company on the ninth day of January was a small blue "2" in the KIA column. Next to the number were the letters "BT" in green pencil, indicating those killed had died from a booby trap. I wondered why the thing that killed the men received a name on the chart, yet they remained a combined number of "2." On the same date there were no numbers in the red column, but listed on the enemy side of the chart near the margin was a small notation in yellow grease pencil that read "1 VN civilian KIA—BT."

I am the only person in the world who remembers that chart for that day. No other members of my platoon were allowed in the command post. The regular staff would have had no reason to remember this one day from all the others. The marks on the chart weren't numbers. They were three people with faces and personalities. Three people I watched die on a small hill in Vietnam. A short time later, I too would be represented by a blue mark on the battalion commander's colorful chart.

You cross a series of lines in war. They aren't drawn in the sand or marked on your maps, yet when you cross one of them you are forever changed. You may never return to what you were before.

The first of these lines is crossed when you participate in the death of another human being. Soldiers can call him the enemy, Viet Cong, Nip, Gook, or whatever they wish, but the fact remains that he was a human being. Look through his bloodstained personal effects, and you are apt to find a letter from home, a picture of a smiling wife and child, or some keepsake you don't understand. As you stare at his lifeless body with curiosity at seeing the first person killed by your own hands, you have lost innocence. You have joined the others in that part of mankind who know they have killed. Because society accepts what you have done in the name of war and expects it, you don't feel an immediate sense of concern. If you are fortunate enough to live many years afterward and experience life's joys, such as one day having grandchildren, you will realize society has given you guilt for taking the life of another person, guilt which it doesn't share with you. You will think of this often.

The second line that you cross in war is to begin accepting injury or death as an everyday occurrence. When you pass the bodies of enemy soldiers killed in the previous night's ambush and give them no more than a curious glance, or when you hear radio reports of another unit requesting an urgent Dust Off for people wounded by a mine and think to yourself that you are glad it was them and not you, then you have lost another part of your humanity. You develop a certain numbness to the events that happen around you in war. You witness so many horrible things that you begin to think that surely nothing any worse than what you have already seen can happen. You have put your men on helicopters with limbs dangling or missing. You have put them in body bags in pieces. Worst of all, you have seen the death of innocent children. You begin to develop a hatred for the people of the country you are supposed to be helping. They are the ones killing and maiming your men.

The third line you cross in war is the one that some of the former members of my platoon had crossed under Lt. William Calley two years earlier at My Lai. At this point, your hatred becomes so intense, paired with your frustration at not being able to retaliate for the deaths of your friends due to the endless mines and booby traps set by the Viet Cong, that you do something that defies common sense. If you had individually asked those men an hour before they entered My Lai if they were capable of shooting an innocent woman or child, each undoubtedly would have responded that it was something he would never do. Yet that is exactly what a few of them did that morning at My Lai. You can reach a point where what you are shooting at is no longer a human being, but simply a target. You lose the ability to pull back and say to yourself, "This is wrong." I know this because of an incident that occurred within my platoon.

We were back on the northern end of the Gaza Strip along the shore of the South China Sea. The pacified village where my men had been killed a few weeks earlier lay a few kilometers to the north. I could see the early morning sun reflecting from the tin roofs. The area where we operated had been cleared of Vietnamese civilians and declared a free-fire zone. Any people spotted there were automatically considered to be Viet Cong, and as such, we were free to engage and kill them.

My platoon was given an assignment to conduct a patrol along the western edge of the Strip along the Cau River, which defined its bor-

der. Nearby, across the river, a group of grass huts formed a small village occupied by a few Vietnamese farmers. We had been assigned
three track-mounted armored personnel carriers (APCs) earlier
that morning by the company commander and were riding atop
them while conducting the patrol.

The terrain along the river was mostly open, sandy ground with
occasional clumps of evergreen trees and other low-growing brush.
From atop the APC, we could see several hundred meters of the
countryside as we moved north along the river. As we approached
the area just south of the small village, one of my men pointed out
a lone figure running west toward the village about five hundred
meters to our right front. The individual carried what appeared to
be a basket, and as we rapidly closed the gap to two hundred meters,
it became obvious the figure was an old woman. She was one hundred meters into the free-fire zone, trying desperately to reach the
river and cross it to get back to her village. A shot rang out from one
of the men on the APC beside me, followed immediately by several
more from other men joining in and firing at the old woman. I
watched as the bullets sprayed the sand around her as she continued
to run. From atop the APC, driving across the rough ground, the
shots were ill aimed, and most flew well over her head. We had
closed the distance to about one hundred meters, and I watched as
the woman threw the basket on the ground and continued to run in
the loose sand toward the river. By now the M-60 machine gun had
joined in on the firing, and I watched as a long burst overtook her.
She was hit and fell down on her knees, only to struggle back to her
feet and continue to hobble toward the river. She had made only a
few steps before she was hit several times, this time never to rise
again. As we pulled next to where her body lay, I could hear whoops
of joy from some of the men. They were excited, as if it had been a
great foxhunt, and they had killed their quarry.

I climbed down from the APC and walked over to the woman's
body. She had been shot through both upper legs and several times

through the upper body. She was old, very old. Her mouth lay agape, and I could see the red betel nut so commonly chewed by Vietnamese women. I walked over to her basket, which contained plant roots the villagers used for food. She had been gathering food. She might have gathered roots from the same spot with her mother as a child, and because someone had decided that she could not go east of the river, we killed her.

Even though I had not fired at her, I was still responsible for her death. I was the officer in charge. A simple command of "cease fire" would have spared her life. We could have easily captured her before she reached the river, yet because we had orders giving us permission to kill, we did. We didn't stop to consider what was happening and make a moral judgment on whether it was right or wrong. We had crossed one of those lines, and we would forever be changed by it.

I dutifully called back to headquarters and reported one Viet Cong killed in action. The old woman would become one of the red grease pencil marks back on LZ Liz in the battalion commander's bunker. When the brigade and division commanders came for their weekly briefings, they wouldn't know that instead of carrying a rifle, this Viet Cong had carried a basket of food. They wouldn't know that she had died terror-filled and wounded, chased by Americans who ran her down on armored personnel carriers. They wouldn't know that across the river the old woman's family had watched her die. They wouldn't know, but I did. It is one of those images Vietnam gave me to carry to my grave.

We continued to move back and forth between the Gaza Strip, 515 Valley, and the mountains. The monsoon season had passed with its nearly constant rain and mud and was replaced by the dry season with its scorching temperatures. Each day was the same. Patrol the area to find the enemy without getting shot or stepping on one of the thousands of mines and booby traps. One day Sergeant Knowles and I calculated the chances of a member of the platoon stepping on a mine or pulling a trip wire hidden in the grass. Two hundred patrols a year, times an average of twenty men in the platoon, times three thousand steps on the average patrol equaled twelve million steps. Twelve million chances for the Viet Cong to figure out where you would put your foot down. They guessed right many times.

When I took command of the platoon, many of the men were getting "short"—nearing the end of their tour. Some rotated to jobs in the rear while others finished their year and made it home. Sergeant Knowles was one of those thinking of going home. Shortly before he left, we did something both of us would remember for the rest of our lives.

We were back in 515 Valley. While on a patrol west of Liz late one afternoon, one of the men spotted a tunnel opening in the side of a small hill. I called Liz and requested two forty-pound shaped charges to blow the tunnel. More than an hour later, a helicopter landed at our position with the explosives and blasting caps. Before dark, we were supposed to link up with the rest of the company fifteen hundred meters to the south. The sun began to drop behind the mountains. I rigged the charges in the mouth of the tunnel after tossing in a couple of grenades. We lit the fuse and backed off, waiting for the explosion. Five minutes, ten minutes, twenty minutes later, and no explosion. I cautiously worked my way back to the tunnel entrance. I had put a five-minute fuse on the charges, but when I looked at them, I saw that the fuse had burned into the blasting cap. Bad cap. I had no more, and we had to get moving. I didn't want to go stumbling south of the river in the dark. We didn't have time for the supply chopper to bring out new caps before dark and still make it to the company night defensive position. Nor did I want to go walking through the thick brush carrying eighty pounds of TNT.

At this point, I came up with the brilliant idea of throwing a hand grenade on the shaped charges and running to the cover of a rice paddy dike forty meters away. I wasn't going to do it by myself. Two grenades, I reasoned, would stand a better chance of detonating the TNT. I looked at Knowles and told him my plan. He wasn't overly enthusiastic about the idea but agreed to go with me. The other men of the platoon watched from a safe distance.

We stood twenty feet from the hole and pulled the pins on our grenades.

"On the count of three," I told him, "pitch the grenade in the hole, and run."

"Okay," he said. "One, two, three."

We tossed the grenades and ran. We didn't stay to see if they went into the tunnel. We ran hard for the paddy dike. Knowles beat me there by a step and dove for cover. Just as we landed, the ground shook, and a tremendous explosion erupted at the tunnel. I started to look over the dike at the effects of the explosion when I glanced up and saw the sky full of dirt clods. They rained down on us. Some of them were as big as my fist. Each time one of them hit Knowles, I heard him grunt. I did the same. In the distance, the men laughed as the dirt clods pelted us. When they stopped falling, we stood and shook the dirt off our backs. Knowles picked up one of the clods and threw it toward the men. They only laughed harder.

He grinned at me. "Let's not do that again," he said.

"I don't think so, either," I said.

We laughed about the incident for several days afterward.

I had been with Charlie Company my entire tour in Vietnam, which was approaching seven months. I had seen enough killing and dying to last a lifetime. I would see much more. The young Viet Cong on the Gaza Strip shot in the throat as he ran toward our position. The two NVA soldiers hiding in a rock cave in the mountains. A rocket from a helicopter gunship hit one of them. Parts of him were scattered over the cave's floor. I shot the other three times with my M-14 as he lay half-hidden behind a large rock in the back of the cave.

If there is any comfort in war, it is in the familiarity and security of the bonds a soldier forms with the men of his unit. My whole world revolved around First Platoon, my platoon. I had heard my men's stories about home, their plans for the future, and the kind

of new car they were going to buy when they got back to the "world."
It is impossible to describe the relationship a soldier forms with
other soldiers, sharing the day-to-day dangers of war. We watched
each other laugh, sometimes cry, and get angry. Together we
endured the heat, the rain, and the cold. We watched each other get
torn and ripped by mines and bullets. And we watched as some died.
I knew the men of First Platoon, Charlie Company well; I trusted
them with my life.

I was bitterly disappointed when I had to leave them.

In February, we were in the southern part of 515 Valley conducting cloverleaf patrols around the river. Captain Donovan called me
on the radio and told me that one of the patrols had found a five-
hundred-pound bomb dropped in an air strike that hadn't
exploded. He gave me the grid coordinates and told me to explode
it in place. The platoon made its way to where the bomb was located
and found it lying on the side of a small hill. I placed a C-4 charge
on the nose of the bomb and attached a ten-minute fuse. We moved
back to the safety of the valley floor to wait for the bomb to explode.

While we were waiting, I got a call from battalion headquarters on
the radio. It was unusual for battalion to use my call sign unless we
were in contact. Normally, messages were relayed through the company commander. They asked for my location. I gave them the coordinates, and they told me to stand by, that a helicopter would be out
in ten minutes to pick me up. I acknowledged the call and handed
the handset back to Stub. The bomb exploded, sending a huge
mushroom of smoke into the air. In the distance back toward Liz, a
helicopter appeared and approached our position. I threw a smoke
grenade on the ground and watched as the helicopter came closer.

"I wonder what they want with me?" I asked Stub.

"Maybe they're giving you a job in the rear," he joked.

"I wouldn't bet on it," I said and walked to where the helicopter
landed a few meters away. It was the last time I saw First Platoon,
Charlie Company.

The chopper lifted off. Instead of heading back to Liz, it turned north across 515 Valley. As we neared the mountains, I saw smoke from a grenade below near a thick stand of trees. The chopper landed, and the co-pilot told me this was my destination. I climbed out, and the helicopter took off back toward Liz. I stood for a moment, watching it slowly disappear. Nearby, a group of soldiers lazed around under the trees. I asked them where the command post was located. They pointed toward the middle of the trees. I saw radio aerials sticking up near the ruins of an old pagoda and headed there. A slender man wearing captain bars met me.

He extended his hand and said, "Lieutenant Bray, I'm Captain Thomas, Alpha Company. I'll be your new company commander."

I was stunned. I asked him if he knew what was going on. He explained that the battalion commander had decided it would be a good idea to switch all the lieutenants in the battalion to different companies. My orders were to take command of Alpha's Second Platoon. No good-byes; no good luck, no see you later. All the respect and confidence I had gained from my platoon was gone. It was like when I had been a kid and had to change schools. Start over again. I didn't like being reassigned to Alpha Company, but like so much of what happened in Vietnam, I accepted it and said, "It don't mean nothing." But it did.

I quickly found that Captain Thomas was a good man and a good soldier. He ran a good company. Like most of the soldiers I served with in Vietnam, the men of Alpha's Second Platoon tried to do their job, survive a year, and go home. Though I kept it to myself, there was only one man in the battalion for whom I had no respect, and he spent each night buried deep in his personal bunker on LZ Liz.

CHAPTER 12

The Most Defining Event

The fourth day of April 1970 began like most of the other days I had spent in Vietnam. Squads returned to Alpha Company's position from overnight ambushes on the trails and travel routes likely used by the North Vietnamese Army or Viet Cong. The company was back in the southern 515 Valley, close to the mountains. The night had been quiet, with none of the snakes reporting contact. As I sat eating my breakfast of cold C rations near a little stream running through the bamboo thickets, I was surprised to hear a helicopter approach our position and land in a nearby clearing. We usually didn't get a supply chopper until afternoon. A few minutes after the helicopter left, Captain Thomas called me on the radio and told me to come over to the command post (CP). He had a mission for my platoon.

The U.S. Army and South Vietnamese government had a number of programs designed to encourage members of the NVA and Viet Cong to defect. The Chieu Hoi, or open-arms, program offered amnesty to Viet Cong soldiers for defecting. My men and I would often see leaflets informing the VC of this option lying in the grass on our patrols. Millions of the flyers were dropped across the area of operations and the mountains. Second Platoon's mission would involve one of these defectors and lead to the most defining event of my tour in Vietnam.

When I arrived at the CP, the "Chieu Hoi," as we called each of the defectors, was sitting on a log next to the company interpreter. He was a fourteen-year-old boy from the village of Duc Pho near the Eleventh Brigade headquarters. He said he had joined the Viet Cong after VC soldiers threatened his family. They had taken him into the hills west of Duc Pho to a small base camp. There, they had kept him for two weeks of political indoctrination and propaganda. Then they assigned him to a unit of the Viet Cong operating near Da Nang, far from his home and family. When the VC gave him the opportunity to tell his family good-bye, he slipped away from the people watching him and turned himself in under the Chieu Hoi program. He carried one of the leaflets in his shirt pocket.

The unfortunate thing for my platoon was that the boy said he could return to the base camp where the Viet Cong had held him, and he was willing to lead us to it. I tried to get him to show us the camp's location on a map so I could plan an approach that would give us an element of surprise, but he babbled to the interpreter, "*No bic, no bic*," which meant "I don't understand." He couldn't read maps. According to the boy, only three or four Viet Cong soldiers usually stayed at the camp, so it would be easy to slip up on them in the surrounding dense brush.

I assembled my platoon, and at 0730 hours we set off, led by our "guide," who insisted the camp was "very close, very close."

We traveled south across the valley floor for more than an hour, and the boy seemed confused about where he was. He kept looking east toward Landing Zone Bronco as if he were trying to get his bearings. We approached the foothills of the mountains. As we passed the burned-out remains of an armored personnel carrier (APC) that had been scarred by many hits from enemy rocket-propelled grenades, the boy stopped and pointed to a low ridge covered by dense brush some five hundred meters to the west. "VC, VC," he repeatedly said. If the Viet Cong base camp was where he said it was, then the soldiers there were already watching us from their elevated position.

The country all around us was open, and the approach to their position was across a small valley with no cover. I had my men spread out at twenty-meter intervals, and we began to cross the valley. At the base of the ridge, the boy moved toward two large black rocks the size of small houses and gestured with his finger up toward the top of the ridge. Between the rocks, through the dense undergrowth, a clearly discernable trail led up the hill. The boy motioned for us to follow him. It was a perfect place for an ambush. If the VC were there, they had had thirty minutes to get ready for us or to flee into the thick jungle behind them. I hoped they had chosen the latter.

There was no way we were going to go up that trail. I told the point man to move fifty meters north along the base of the ridge to find an opening up the hill. He found an area where we could go up, and we began moving toward some large rocks that were visible up the ridge about one hundred meters away. We crossed a small streambed below the rocks and saw the first evidence of possible Viet Cong presence: a couple of discarded C ration cans lying in the stream. The Viet Cong often ate American C rations they got on the black market near U.S. base camps. But the most potent evidence of VC presence near the stream was the smell—the same sweet, half-sickening odor of cooked rice, incense, smoke, and sweat found in Vietnamese villages. The VC were close, or they had been. I motioned for the leader of the point squad to stop as I moved to his position. We were below a huge rock surrounded by dense brush. The small stream ran around the rock, and I whispered to the squad leader to follow it up the hill and to watch closely for ambushes and booby traps.

We rounded the large rock. Tucked into a small, flat piece of ground barely twenty feet square lay the VC camp, but there was no sign of the Viet Cong. They had seen us coming and fled into the jungle behind the camp. I posted security around the camp and told the rest of the platoon to take a break.

It was 1000 hours. The temperature had climbed rapidly. I began looking around the area, ever aware of the possibility of booby traps.

It was an ideal spot for a base camp. The small stream running ten feet away provided ample water, and the trees overhead and the large rocks surrounding the camp made it impossible to spot from the air. A couple of small pits had been dug near the center of the camp for fires, and there was evidence of recent cooking. To one side of the pits lay a bundle of dried grass and sticks for fuel. There were three hooches with sleeping positions for up to eight men per hooch. Some of them even had mosquito netting. These people had it better out there than we did, I thought. The hooches had raised floors. Underneath one of them, we found clothing, canteen cups, a fully loaded M-16 magazine with twenty rounds, and a handwritten poster.

When I asked the interpreter what the poster said, he laughed.

"Poster say for GI to Chieu Hoi," he said.

Either the VC it belonged to had a hell of a sense of humor, or he was extremely dedicated to his cause. I couldn't imagine any American wanting to join the Viet Cong. One of the squad leaders came up from off the perimeter and told me one of his men had found an observation platform in the top of a tree fifty meters southeast of the base camp.

The Chieu Hoi moved about the camp, pointing and jabbering in Vietnamese. He put his hands together on the side of his head in a sleeping motion and pointed to one of the rice straw mats lying in one of the hooches, indicating where he had slept.

To the rear of the camp, next to one of the large rocks, steps had been built from smaller rocks, which allowed us to climb to the top of the larger rock. From there, the disappearance of the Viet Cong was no longer in doubt. I could clearly see the valley we had crossed and all the surrounding terrain, except the jungle behind the camp. In the distance, I could see the APC where the boy had finally figured out his location. I climbed down the rock and asked the interpreter where the Viet Cong had gone. After a talk with the boy, he said the Viet Cong had another camp a short walk away and gestured toward the west and the dense jungle. He said there were caves at the other camp.

I called Captain Thomas and reported what we had found at the camp and the possibility of another some distance away. He told me to check the surrounding area for five hundred meters to the north, and if we didn't find anything, to return to the company position. I requested a Warlord team to fly overhead. An observation helicopter and a couple of Cobra gunships would make me feel better about looking for the caves that were supposed to be ahead. I already knew the VC were close by. Before we left the camp, I marked its position on my map. When we were clear of the area, I was going to request an air strike on the location from one of the Helix forward air controllers who worked our area. A few canisters of napalm dropped on the camp would ensure the Viet Cong didn't use it again. I assembled the platoon, feeling lucky that we had not detonated a mine or been ambushed.

We were leaving the camp in a different direction than we had arrived, so I decided to go nearer the point to pick out a good route to take us north and eventually back to the company. I arranged the platoon in two parallel lines about thirty meters apart to keep from getting scattered in the dense cover ahead. We would move forward one hundred meters to the crest of a small ridge and then wait for the Warlord team to arrive.

We moved north along the slope of the ridge through intermittent waist-high brush. We were approximately fifty meters from the base camp. I glanced up the ridge to the left when a bolt of lightning and the loudest clap of thunder I had ever heard hit twenty feet in front of me, or so it seemed. One second I was looking up the ridge, the next I was lying flat on my back, staring up at the blue sky and watching a dark gray mushroom cloud rising slowly upward. We had had no warning. No metallic click, no thud from a grenade hitting the ground, only the deafening sound of a huge explosion. There was no gunfire signaling an ambush. I heard someone moaning

ahead of me and wondered how many of my men were hurt. I had
to get up and see. I rolled over on my right side and looked down at
the top of my right wrist. Every time my heart beat, a stream of blood
squirted out of it onto the ground. One, two, three times I watched.
I put my left hand over the hole and squeezed. Still no gunfire. No
ambush.

I heard exclamations—"Damn!" and "Medic."

I pushed myself onto my knees with my elbows and instinctively
searched for my rifle. It was ten feet ahead of me. How did it get up
there, I wondered. Then I realized it didn't get up there; I had gotten back here. I rose to get my rifle in case shooting started. As I
stood, a nauseated feeling hit me in the pit of my stomach. Something was wrong. I took one step and nearly fell to my right. I looked
down, and my right leg was soaked with blood. A small stream of it
ran out on top of my boot. I could see a round hole in the top of my
right front pants pocket, but I felt no pain.

My radio-telephone operator (RTO) was directly behind me. I
asked him if he was okay.

"I think," he answered.

I could see the point man lying ten meters in front of me. The
backs of both of his legs were soaked in blood. The platoon medic
was helping a man to my right. There was still no machine gun, rifle,
or rocket-propelled grenade (RPG) fire. No ambush. We had detonated a mine or booby trap. I told the platoon sergeant to establish
a perimeter. A couple of the men went to treat the point man's
wounds. They ripped his fatigue pants to reveal several holes in the
back of his legs. He also had blood soaking his shirt from wounds in
his back. The man to my right had wounds in his chest, face, and
groin. Two other men were being helped—one wounded in the
right arm, the other hit in the hip and arm.

The RTO tied a sterile bandage around my wrist. With my other
hand, I reached for the radio handset on his back. I called the company and requested an urgent Dust Off for five U.S. wounded in

action and gave our grid coordinates. As we waited for the Dust Off
to arrive, I hobbled over to where the mine had exploded. From the
size of the crater and the radius of the area in which shrapnel had
hit people, I assumed it was an 81 mm mortar round. There were no
signs of a trip wire, and the explosion had occurred slightly to our
right, so the point man couldn't have stepped on it. It might have
been command detonated by a Viet Cong soldier lying in the brush
ahead.

In the distance I could hear the popping of rotor blades as the Dust
Off approached our position. I called the pilot on the radio and gave
him directions to our location. We were on the side of the ridge, but
the slope didn't allow him to touch down and land. I asked him if he
wanted us to move to a better location, and he responded that he
could make it where we were. As he hovered a couple of feet above the
ground, I helped load the other wounded men and climbed in after
them, using the runners underneath the helicopter for steps. I told
the platoon sergeant to call Captain Thomas to tell him that he, the
sergeant, was in charge of the platoon.

As the helicopter gained altitude and turned for the short flight
to the brigade field hospital at Bronco, one of the onboard medics
asked me where I had been hit. I showed him my wrist and pointed
to the blood-soaked hole in my pocket. He used a pair of scissors to
cut my pants and exposed a hole the size of a dime oozing blood
down the side of my leg. He placed a bandage over it and told me to
apply pressure until we reached the aid station. I glanced at my
watch—1155 hours. I wondered why there was no pain. I thought
back to the explosion and had no memory of the projectiles hitting
me. I had seen many men wounded during my time in Vietnam.
Some would scream in agony while others would quietly ask how
badly they were hit.

The helicopter landed just outside the aid station. The two
worst-wounded men were put on stretchers and carried inside. The
rest of us limped along behind. I was greeted at the door by the

sight of two black body bags lying in the hall. They weren't empty. Ahead, there were two trails of blood drops on the white floor leading to rooms where my two men had been taken. A young soldier in fatigues busied himself with a mop and a bucket of water, cleaning up the blood.

I walked past the body bags, and an orderly guided me into one of the small rooms. Inside was a large metal table with a light hanging overhead. The orderly placed me on the table on my back and began removing the bandages from my wrist and hip. One of the doctors removed a cotton swab with a long handle from its package and dipped it into a bottle of yellow fluid. He wiped the blood from the wound in my hip and inserted the swab nearly four inches into my upper leg. Now I had pain. He said the projectile hadn't hit any major blood vessels or bone, and that my leg would be fine. He then examined my wrist and ordered x-rays before leaving the room. When he returned, he told me there was possible damage to the nerves and tendons in my wrist, and that he was sending me to the division hospital at Chu Lai for further examination. I asked him about the condition of my men, and he said that a couple of them were also being flown to Chu Lai for treatment. None of their injuries was life threatening.

At Chu Lai, the doctors examined my wounds and determined that there was no permanent damage. They opened the entry wounds and made them larger with scalpels and said the best thing to do was to leave the shrapnel inside because it would do more harm than good to remove it. They assigned me a bunk in a nearby barracks, and I reported to the aid station each day for a week for them to check my wounds and change the dressings. My leg was stiff for a few days, but I hobbled around on a pair of crutches. On a few occasions I went to the nearby officers' club and was offered many drinks by the pilots and staff officers stationed at Chu Lai.

At the end of the week, I was released to go back to Bronco and was given one more week of light duty. I hoped to get a job in the rear. Most officers only spent six to seven months in the field and then transferred to a staff or support job. But it wasn't to be. After my week of light duty, I was flown back to the Gaza Strip aboard the supply helicopter. I was a platoon leader again.

Shortly after I rejoined Alpha Company, we moved to Liz for the monthly rotation. One day the battalion executive officer, a major, walked down to the bunker line and told me he wanted to talk to me. We went outside, and he told me the colonel wanted to know if I would take command of Recon Platoon, which was under the battalion commanding officer's supervision. It was the best assignment in the battalion for a lieutenant. All the men were volunteers for the platoon, and they had a reputation of being a close-knit and efficient unit. If I had been offered the job six months earlier, I would have taken it immediately. Now, I had ninety days left in country, and the thought of being under the direct supervision of the colonel didn't appeal to me at all.

I had recently had an experience with him that had caused me to like him even less. Orders had come down promoting me to first lieutenant. Someone at Bronco had changed the insignia on my shirt collars from second lieutenant to first lieutenant, but I wasn't even aware it had been done. While we were on Liz, the colonel called me up to the command bunker. When he saw the first lieutenant bars on my collar, he went into a rage and said that I wasn't a goddamned first lieutenant until he promoted me. I tried to explain to him that I had nothing to do with sewing the insignia on my collar. He pinned the silver bar on my shirt and stormed back into the bunker. I wondered why a man like that had been given command of troops. I told the major that I didn't want the job.

The day before Alpha Company left Liz to go back into the field, a company formation was called on the heliport near the command bunker. American and battalion flags blew in the breeze. Streamers from all the battles the battalion had fought in over the last hundred years were attached to the battalion flag. As we stood in formation, I was surprised to hear my name, along with two other soldiers' names, called to come forward. The colonel gave a short speech to the assembled men, and then his aide read a citation from Captain Thomas awarding me a Bronze Star.

The aide then read another citation. This time, he said, "First Lieutenant Gary Bray, you are hereby awarded the Purple Heart for wounds inflicted by a hostile enemy of the United States."

The colonel pinned the medals to my shirt pocket and moved down the line to decorate the other two soldiers. When the formation was dismissed and the colonel went to his bunker, I stood for a moment gazing down at the medals shining in the bright morning sun. I was proud. Very proud. I stared at the shiny Purple Heart and remembered the times my cousins and I had sneaked into my uncle's bedroom to look at this same medal, now hanging on my chest. People would be proud of me for serving my country, as they had been of my uncle and the men who had served during World War II. I would keep these medals so that someday my son and nephews could look at them and be proud of me, as I had been of my uncle.

Over the next months, the company continued to do the things I had done for almost a year. People kept dying, and we continued to call Dust Offs on nearly a daily basis. But I could sense a change. The morale was different than when I had arrived almost twelve months earlier. The mood of the men had changed. Rumors persisted about units going home. What we quickly realized was that the soldiers weren't going home—only their unit flags were leaving, accompanied by a small token staff. Instead of going home with the flags, soldiers who had any time left on their tour were simply reassigned to a unit that was staying. Understandably, they weren't happy. I began to hear more and more reports from the replacements that things were getting worse. Stories of race riots at Da Nang, fragging—or assassination—of officers in the rear, and outright mutiny from companies that refused to obey orders in the field were becoming more and more common. I missed First Platoon, Charlie Company. Things had been different with them.

It seemed unreal. I sat in the battalion rear on Landing Zone Bronco and realized that in nine days I would be back in Oklahoma, away from this place where I had spent the last year watching as so many people were maimed and killed. In the meantime, though, Alpha Company was about to be airlifted into the jungle once again.

Captain Thomas looked at me and said, "You got nine days left; do you want to get on a helicopter and get out of here?"

I didn't hesitate. I was going home. I had survived Vietnam. I had fought in a war for my country and was proud of the way I had conducted myself. Surely no one could ask more of me.

A few days later, the C-130 flight from LZ Bronco to Chu Lai was scheduled for 1000 hours. I was at the airstrip at 0700. I didn't want to miss the flight that would start my long journey home. The day before, I had turned in all my equipment and collected my personal belongings that had been in the locker for a year. The company sergeant who had helped me so much when I arrived had long since returned home. I felt sad when I placed my M-14 in the rack at the company armory. I had carried it every step I had taken for the last year. As I placed it in the rack, I remembered the first person I had ever aimed it at and pulled the trigger. The rifle and I had seen a lot together.

A warrant officer I had become acquainted with walked into the little building where I sat waiting for my flight. During the week I spent at Bronco on light duty, I had flown with him on a couple of occasions to deliver mail to the remote firebases in the brigade's area of operations. He asked me where I was going, and I told him I was going home, waiting for a flight to Chu Lai.

"I'm headed that way," he said. "Want a ride?"

"You bet," I answered.

It was two hours before the C-130 was due to arrive. I told the sergeant at the flight desk I was hitching a ride on the chopper. I threw my duffel bag in the back of the two-man light observation helicopter, and we started north up Highway 1. I looked for the last time toward the mountains behind 515 Valley. They were shrouded in mist. I couldn't see the ridge where I had been wounded.

We flew over the access road to Liz. Below I could see a team of engineers with their metal detectors sweeping the one-lane paved road for mines. Two days later, Charlie Company would travel down that road, returning to Liz from an operation on the river to the north. As I later found out, the men were in good spirits. They had just killed three Viet Cong and captured their weapons. The company would normally have been picked up by helicopter, but on that day all the helicopters were being used for a large combat assault by one of the other battalions. The men had walked to Highway 1 to be picked up by trucks for the trip to Liz.

That day, Sherman Armstrong, the young man who had teased me about the high school football games, rode in the cab of the lead truck with Charlie Company's new commander, Lieutenant Nelson. Armstrong was one of the last original members of my platoon remaining in the field. A job in the rear awaited his arrival at Liz. He would go home in fifty-four days. The week before, a job in the rear had come open in supply. He and John Smith were eligible for the position. They flipped a coin, and Smith won. Now another job was open, and Armstrong had gotten it. He was looking forward to getting out of the field and returning to Oklahoma.

At 1445 hours, the lead truck turned off Highway 1 for the one-mile ride to Liz. Armstrong had it made; he could see Liz straight ahead. To the side, a couple of Vietnamese kids played in the fields that lined the road. A village lay nearby in a stand of bamboo and banana trees. The two and a half ton truck picked up speed. With a half mile to go, the truck hit a mine and was thrown high into the air. The engine and back wheels were blown off and went flying. The truck landed fifty feet from a five-foot crater in the access road. Lieutenant Nelson was dead. Armstrong had just minutes to live. Twenty-seven other soldiers, who were riding in the back of the truck, were injured. The two Vietnamese kids ran toward the village. They were caught and later admitted that the Viet Cong who lived in the village had shown them how to detonate the mine when the truck reached a point marked on the road. Recon Platoon's search of the deserted village resulted only in the horrible wounding of one of its members by a booby trap the villagers had set before they fled.

Two days before all that came to pass, the warrant officer and I continued our flight up Highway 1. To the east, bulldozers were busy clearing the brush from the Gaza Strip. We passed over the red-dirt access road for whose construction Embree and Wade had given their lives. A few Vietnamese people walked down the road carrying baskets on bamboo poles, wearing their conical rice straw hats. There were no vehicle tracks, only a well-worn footpath down the middle of the road. We flew on to Chu Lai. I didn't want to see any more of the mountains, 515 Valley, or the Gaza Strip.

The rice paddies, fields, and mountains of the southern part of the 515 Valley form the background as I have my picture taken. The weapons on my utility belt indicate that even in such picturesque spots, you couldn't let your guard down.

A small village in 515 Valley, just before we moved the people out—and burned the village.

Left, Len Groom and *right,* Harold Ruffin cleaning an M-60 machine gun. Len was a big, quiet Minnesota kid who had become a welder after high school before he was drafted. He started as a rifleman but wound up as a machine gunner.

Foreground, Sergeant Knowles; *middle,* Steve "Stub" Fordice, my RTO (radioman); and *background,* Steve "Doc" Miles, the platoon medic, relax in a Vietnam village.

A crew constructs a road to a village as part of a program known as the "Strategic Hamlet Initiative." Under the program, selected villages considered loyal to the South Vietnamese were provided with permanent housing within a defensive perimeter. In the background, where the bulldozer sits on the hill, is where Wade, Embree, and the child were killed by a land mine.

Sherman "Bo" Armstrong and I grew up barely forty miles from each other. He liked to kid me about the fact that his high school had always beaten mine in football. With fifty-four days remaining of his tour in Vietnam, Bo was killed by a roadside mine detonated by children.

This is the photo I took of three soldiers that is similar to one Boyd Wade's brother has in his home in Ringling, Oklahoma. In the version of the photograph I shot that belongs to Gary Wade, Boyd sits in the vacant spot on the left beside his transistor radio, boots, and M-60 machine gun, which appear here. Sherman Armstrong is on the left in this photograph.

157

The Purple Heart and Bronze Star are pinned on my uniform. This was a moment I'll never forget. The Purple Heart had intrigued me ever since I was a boy back in Oklahoma, where I had admired the Purple Heart awarded to my uncle Olen for his service in World War II.

CHAPTER 13

Leaving Vietnam

Leaving Vietnam was strangely like arriving. As the wheels of the charter jet lifted from the soil of Vietnam to take other soldiers and me back to America, a loud cheer erupted. Then an eerie silence fell as each man reflected on what he had experienced over the last year. On our way to Vietnam we had wondered what the coming year would bring. Now each of us carried the images, forever etched in our minds, of what Vietnam had been. It was history, unchangeable. Memories, whether good or bad, would remain with us until we died. Our service in Vietnam had become the most important thing we would ever do in our lives. No experience could remove it from the center of who we were. While marriage, children, and careers are the central factors of most people's experiences, for those of us on that flight home, that year in our early lives would never move aside and let us be the normal people everyone expected us to become. The events of the coming years would ensure that Vietnam would never go away for those of us who served there.

I came back to America via Seattle, Washington. I never gave my reception much thought until I heard about the returning soldiers at Los Angeles being spit on and called baby killers. As I made my way through the terminal to board the flight that would take me home, not one person spoke to me or smiled. They avoided looking at me. I was still wearing the jungle fatigues and boots I had worn in Vietnam, yet no one seemed to notice. Imagine the elation I felt upon returning home after a year in a place where every day I could have been killed, only to have people ignore me.

There was no adjustment period or quiet place to go to get used to the idea that I was no longer in a place where people were trying to kill me. One night I was sleeping in Vietnam and the next I was back in America, safe in my hometown. That first night back home I would close my eyes, but I hadn't left Vietnam behind. Each little noise would bring me to instant alertness. The closing of a door, the barking of a dog, and the sound of a tree limb rubbing the house were the noises that I had to get reacquainted with. They had been danger signals for the last year, but now all that was over. I was physically safe.

I was proud of what I had accomplished. In the three years since I graduated from high school, I had became an officer in the United States Army, led a platoon of men for a year in a war, and received a Purple Heart and a Bronze Star for heroism. At the time I didn't realize it, but aside from my immediate family and me, few people in America were proud of me or the hundreds of thousands of men who had served our country in Vietnam. We would be portrayed as people who had made a huge mistake.

"Vietnam was wrong."

"America should have never gotten involved in another country's civil war."

"We're killing innocent civilians."

I would soon hear those comments on television from politicians who wanted to distance themselves from what had happened in Vietnam. I didn't have the luxury of distancing myself. Vietnam had a permanent home in the center of who I was to be for the rest of my life. I could push the war aside or cover it with other thoughts and emotions, yet the images would never go away or diminish in their clarity.

I came home from Vietnam with a need to share my experience with others and understand that what I had endured had accomplished something. What I quickly learned was that it was best not to mention the fact that I was a Vietnam veteran. It was hard to understand that when I talked to my former high school friends it was best not to bring up the subject. They were aware that I had just returned home from the army. They knew my wife and family had been notified when I had been wounded, yet at the mention of the word "Vietnam," friends looked embarrassed or quickly changed the subject. It was as though they thought if we didn't talk about it, Vietnam would go away.

All these decades later, the response from members of my generation is still the same. Bring up the subject of Vietnam with a group of fifty- to sixty-year-old men and the atmosphere of the conversation changes immediately. Each of those men lives with the decisions he made in his youth. Some married to avoid the draft, some took college deferments, some went to Canada, and some went to war. Of those who went to war, fifty-eight thousand Americans died and countless other thousands like myself were wounded.

Ringling, Oklahoma, 2002 II

I opened the glass storm door and stepped into the small living room of the white wood house. The old man inside reminded me of my own father who had died just two years earlier—the wrinkled skin on the hand he offered to shake as we greeted each other, the frail appearance of one who has lived for eighty-eight years. I asked him if he was Mr. Wade, and he said yes.

"Did you have a son named Boyd who was killed in Vietnam?" I asked.

"Yes," he replied.

"My name is Gary Bray. I was his platoon leader in Vietnam. I was with him when he was killed."

"You were?" he said.

"Yes, sir, my wife and I were passing through Ringling and I stopped and visited his grave at the cemetery."

"That's his picture there on the shelf," he said, pointing to a small bookshelf on the wall.

I saw the picture of Boyd that had been taken when he graduated from high school. Next to his photograph, Purple Heart, Bronze Star, and Vietnam Service medals were kept in a frame.

I asked him if those were Boyd's medals.

"Yes," he said. He reached over to the table next to him and picked up another frame that contained two medals, one green and one orange. "These are my medals," he said as he proudly handed them to me.

As I looked at them, the phone rang.

"There is a man here you need to talk to," he said into the phone. "No, his wife is in the car, and he won't be here long, so come on down." He turned to me and said, "That was Boyd's brother, and he will be right here. He wants to talk to you."

I looked out the door at the driveway and wondered what it would have been like thirty-two years ago when the green army sedan pulled up outside their home. Did they see the car pull into the driveway and the men get out with a telegram in hand? Fifty-eight thousand times this had happened to a wife, a mother and father, or a brother or sister.

I held the medals and wondered if Boyd had admired them as a small boy, as I had admired those of my uncle during my childhood. Had he also heard the stories of war? Had the medals and the stories instilled in him at an early age the idea that to serve your country was an honorable thing?

I handed the medals back to Mr. Wade as a white pickup pulled in the driveway. As he approached the door, Mr. Wade explained that was his other son and he pointed to the pictures on the shelf and the high school photograph of the man who was opening the front door.

"Gary Wade," Boyd's brother said as we shook hands.

"Hello, Mr. Wade," I said and explained to him that I had been his brother's platoon leader and that I had been with Boyd when he was killed.

Gary told me his family had contacted the army several times to find out the circumstances surrounding Boyd's death, but all they had ever been told was that he had been killed by an enemy mine. I answered his questions concerning what had happened that morning, how Boyd and Embree had been sharing their C rations with the children from a nearby village and how the mine had killed Boyd, Embree, and one of the kids. Gary wanted to know if Boyd had died instantly or had suffered. I told him that Boyd had died within a minute of the explosion. Gary spoke proudly of his brother, telling me that the funeral had been the biggest ever in the county. He told me that Boyd had been stout as a bull in high school, and that he could throw a dime into the air and shoot it with a .22 caliber rifle. He spoke from the fond memories of a little brother.

Gary told me he had a picture of Boyd from Vietnam at his house and that he wanted to show it to me. He thought I might know the other two people in the picture with his brother. I said good-bye to Boyd's father and followed Gary the few blocks to his house. We went inside, and there in the hallway was a ten-by-fourteen photograph of Boyd and two other young soldiers sitting on some rocks in a small Vietnamese village.

I recognized the picture instantly. I had taken it. I remembered Boyd asking me to take the picture for him. I had one identical to it at home, only in the place where Boyd was sitting there was another soldier. I couldn't remember the names of the two other people in the picture with Boyd but told Gary that I had some photographs of Boyd at home that I would make copies of and send to him.

He gave me his address and thanked me for stopping to visit with him and his father. I told him that I hoped my visit had not caused him or his father pain by bringing back the events of so long ago, but that after visiting Boyd's grave and finding out that his father was still alive, I had wanted to talk to him. I had wanted to let him know that there was someone else with whom the memory of Boyd lived, and that it had been an honor to have known him.

I think often of that grave in Ringling, Oklahoma. How on a day in January 1970, the report of rifles firing across it and the lonely sound of taps playing in the far corner of the cemetery signaled the final good-bye to a young boy. How on that same day, halfway around the world, other young men were put into body bags by those who would survive and return home to live with the memories of a war that America would try to forget. America can forget Vietnam, but those of us with its memories will only forget when we too finally lie under a stone in some place like the cemetery in Ringling, Oklahoma.